BARRON'S
EZ-101
STUDY KEYS

..._m, Ph.D.
Senior Statistical Researcher
NOVA Research Company

Sociology

BARRON'S

All inquiries should be addressed to:
Barron's Educational Series, Inc.
250 Wireless Boulevard
Hauppauge, NY 11788

Library of Congress Catalog Card No. 91-33790

International Standard Book No. 0-8120-4853-9

Library of Congress Cataloging-in-Publication Data

Klein, Hugh.
  Sociology / Hugh Klein.
    p. cm. — (Barron's EZ 101 study keys)
  Includes index.
  ISBN 0-8120-4853-9
    1. Sociology. 2. Sociology—Research— Methodology.   I. Title.
  II. Series
HM51.K56 1991
301—dc20   91-33790
                                                                                    CIP

PRINTED IN THE UNITED STATES OF AMERICA
2345 5500 98765432

CONTENTS

Theme 1 WHAT IS SOCIOLOGY?

*T*he primary purpose of Theme 1 is to explain what sociology is and what sociology, as an academic discipline, does. In addition to giving a definition (and an accompanying explanation of the definition) of sociology, this theme compares sociology to several other social sciences. The emphasis here is to demonstrate to the reader how sociology has made its own unique contribution to contemporary understanding of the social world in which we live.

INDIVIDUAL KEYS IN THIS THEME	
1	Sociology defined and explained
2	Sociology vs. psychology
3	Sociology vs. anthropology
4	Sociology vs. social work
5	Sociology vs. political science
6	Sociology vs. economics
7	Sociology vs. the new disciplines (women's studies, urban studies)

Key 1 Sociology defined and explained

OVERVIEW *Sociology is the scientific study of human societies and social behavior.*

Scientific study: As in other scientific studies, sociological investigations proceed **systematically**. Like other scientists, sociologists begin their work by proposing questions of importance to them, and then designing a research project that will enable them to ascertain the answers to their major research questions. Just as chemists conduct experiments that are unique to their discipline with various compounds, or behavioral psychologists conduct learning-type experiments unique to their discipline with rats, sociologists have their own specific ways of trying to discover the answers to questions of importance to them. As a **social science**, sociology is a discipline that is **organized** and **methodical**, and its endeavors are undertaken for the purpose of **enhancing knowledge**.

Human societies: Sociologists examine **humans**, in particular, **groups of humans**, in an effort to understand the nature, meaning, and significance of human group relationships. Two distinctions are made:
- A distinction between human and animal societies:
  Sociologists are only interested in understanding things relevant to the human experience. Sociology can be distinguished from anthropology or psychology in that the latter disciplines occasionally examine nonhuman animal species, whereas sociologists do not.
- A distinction between studying **individuals** and studying **groups** or the interaction patterns of many groups:
  Individuals are not the focus of sociology except when they are in a social context; groups are the focus of sociology.

Social behavior: Sociologists examine the things that people do that affect others around them, or the things that people do after they have given thought to how others might respond to their acts, especially when the people are aggregated into groups. Sociology seeks to understand how groups work, how groups influence one another, and how groups influence the things that individuals do.

Key 2 Sociology vs. psychology

OVERVIEW *Sociology and psychology share the common goal of trying to understand and explain human behavior, but they are different from one another in their primary goals. Psychology attempts to explain how and why **individuals** act, or how **individuals** influence others' behavior. Sociology attempts to explain how and why **groups** act, or how **groups** influence individuals' behaviors.*

Scope of focus: The focus of psychology is narrower or smaller (the individual vs. group), but **not** less important than that of sociology.

Biological or biochemical factors: Some psychologists consider people's behaviors to be influenced by chemicals in the brain that affect moods and emotions. Most sociologists would not be concerned with these factors. They are more interested in the effects of **interpersonal, cultural**, and **subcultural influences** on behavior.

Motivation: Psychology and sociology also differ in the way they typically attempt to answer the question, "Why did a person perform an action?"
- Sociologists would approach this question by looking at **social factors** that influence behaviors. They would ordinarily focus on how such variables as membership in a particular group, social class, gender, or race shape a person's actions.
- Some psychologists would consider an individual's specific, **personal** motivations for engaging in an action. The psychologist asks what people think about their actions.

Explanations of human behavior: A comprehensive explanation of human behavior must utilize the explanations offered by both psychology and sociology.
- To utilize a **sociological** approach without considering the pertinent psychological data is to run the risk of assuming incorrectly that people are merely acted upon by their environments, and that the things they do are shaped exclusively by external forces.
- To utilize a **psychological** approach without considering the pertinent sociological data is to run the risk of assuming incorrectly that people are able to act entirely of their own accord, without regard to the external forces around them.

Key 3 Sociology vs. anthropology

OVERVIEW *Sociology and anthropology have many similarities and differences. Both fields of study strive to understand human behavior, and both disciplines approach their study at the aggregate (group) level. One branch of anthropology,* **cultural anthropology***, shares an interest with sociology in its focus on cultural issues. The other branches of anthropology,* **archaeology** *and* **physical anthropology***, are different from sociology in their examination, respectively, of relics and skeletal remains to understand peoples of the past.*

Archaeology: This branch of anthropology examines **relics** of peoples and civilizations past (for example, their books, pottery fragments, building remains) in an effort to derive an understanding of how these peoples lived and how their societies functioned. In contrast, while some sociologists also have an interest in understanding **peoples** and **civilizations** of the past, they would not typically undertake their academic endeavors by examining relics.

Physical anthropology: This branch of anthropology studies and tries to understand what it means to be a human being by studying **evolutionary predecessors** of human beings (for example, *Homo erectus*, "Neanderthal man").

- Skeletal remains are examined in an effort to understand how primitive humans lived.
- Physical anthropologists try to discover and explain the significance of such traits as larger or smaller cranial capacities or greater numbers of molar teeth, and what such traits, typically found in prehuman human beings but not in modern-day human beings, indicate regarding how these ancestors of humans lived their lives.
- This type of questioning and knowledge is not of interest to sociologists.

Cultural anthropology: This discipline is the branch of anthropology that is most like sociology. It addresses the same fundamental questions as sociology:

- How are humans shaped by their culture, and how do they, in turn, influence the culture around them?

- Of what does a particular group's culture consist?
- What sorts of folkways, norms, formal rules, groups, and institutions characterize a group's daily life?
- Despite sharing an interest in the study of cultural issues, cultural anthropologists and sociologists are often interested in slightly different **questions**, and they are apt to adhere to slightly different **assumptions** about human cultural systems.

Key 4 Sociology vs. social work

OVERVIEW *Sociology and social work are concerned about many of the same **issues** but their primary **purposes** are completely different. Sociology's primary purpose is to conduct research into the social world by developing and testing theoretical models to explain various social phenomena, whereas social work's primary purpose is to alleviate social problems.*

Research vs. application:
- Sociology is oriented toward the research and theoretical aspects of human group relations, social work toward the applied aspects of human group relations.
- Sociologists try to improve the world by learning about its peoples and their cultures, and then sharing their knowledge about the world's problems.
- Sociologists are typically involved in doing research and working with theories or conceptual models that explain the social world, but they do little about the problems they discover or the phenomena that they explain or uncover.
- Social workers try to improve the world with firsthand involvement, with hands-on experience in dealing with "real world" social problems.

Example: A sociologist and a social worker may both be interested in child abuse.
- The sociologist may **conduct a study** to determine how prevalent child abuse is in America, what factors are related to abusiveness, and which types of children are most at risk. Once this study has been completed, the sociologist will probably write some articles for professional journals or perhaps a book on the subject, reporting the findings to others in the scholarly community.
- The social worker, on the other hand, wants to **do something specific** to change and improve the lot of America's abused children.
  1. The social worker may meet with abused children, their families and friends, or other interested parties, and try to **intervene** in the cycle of abuse.

2. Through a combination of problems assessment (for example, discovering the relevant abusiveness, codependency, violence in a particular family), counseling, and references to community resources, the social worker tries to make a **personal** difference in the problem of child abuse.

Interactive disciplines: Were it not for sociological research, much would not be learned about social problems. Were it not for social work, much would go unchanged in the world. Sociology and social work are interactive disciplines, similar to sociology and psychology (see Key 2). Sociology points the **direction** for social work; then social work tries to do something **positjve** about the problems it tackles.

Key 5 Sociology vs. political science

OVERVIEW *Although sociology and political science are studied separately by people identifying themselves as either sociologists or political scientists, political science falls under the domain of sociology. Political science deals with **social** process of the same kind that sociologists study.*

*In order to have a political, or governing, system, people must organize themselves into a **group**, decide what is in their best interests, and then determine how to go about ensuring that these interests are pursued and upheld. Anytime political scientists examine the political sphere of social relations, they are studying something that is of interest to sociologists.*

Four subject areas of political science that are sociological:

- Political science studies **behavior** related to the functioning of the governmental system. Examples are lobbying groups or voting tendencies of certain social groups.
- Some political scientists are interested in understanding more about the **interrelationship** among popular attitudes, values, and social policy. Examples include how the public's attitudes about abortion are mobilized into efforts to legalize or criminalize abortion, or how American citizens' beliefs about homosexuality are reflected in laws regarding gay and lesbian rights.
- Political science also entails scientific examinations of **group membership characteristics**, in an effort to understand how group dynamics and demographic composition influence the group's political activities. The political scientist might wish to understand, for example, how black and white members belonging to a particular group try to persuade other group members to pursue their specific goals, or how men and women members differ from one another in terms of their group participation in political groups.
- Political scientists may study decision-making **policies**, **practices**, and **tendencies** in an effort to understand how laws get passed, what concerns go into the law-making process, and what obstacles are faced in the official process of law making.

Political science and political sociology: Political science most closely resembles sociology when the phenomena being considered fall into what is usually referred to by sociologists as **political sociology**, which is a subdiscipline in the larger field of sociology.

- Other subfields in sociology are of virtually no interest or relevance to political scientists (for example, microsociology, which is the study of face-to-face social interactions).
- Conversely, sociologists study the **political implications of human behavior**, but in ways that have little to do with the primary disciplinary interest of political scientists.

Key 6 Sociology vs. economics

OVERVIEW *Of all of the social sciences, economics differs most from sociology.*

Economics definition: Economics is a discipline concerned with studying the **production**, **distribution**, and **consumption** of goods (for example, textiles, agricultural products, mining output). It is considered a social science because the goods that are produced are a reflection of **groups** of people's wants and needs, and the specific groups that purchase or use particular goods also tend to fall into certain identifiable social patterns.

Differences: Many of the phenomena studied in economics such as money flow, the fiscal health of a nation or organization, product distribution, commodities manufacturing, product availability, and product accessibility, are not of much interest to sociologists.

Similarities: When commodities-related issues are of interest to sociologists, the sociologists are much more likely to concern themselves with social trends.

KEY EXAMPLE

Consumerism deals with such matters as which specific groups (for example, young people, urban dwellers) are the greatest consumers of a particular product, what in the surrounding culture influences them to demand certain goods and not others, and how the use of certain products reflects upon and subsequently influences the society-at-large.

Interactive disciplines: To comprehend fully what production of a particular commodity is all about, it is beneficial to examine both aspects of consumerism—the manufacturer and the purchaser, the distributor and the consumer—and to utilize some of the main principles of **both** economics and sociology.

Key 7 Sociology vs. the new disciplines (women's studies, urban studies)

OVERVIEW *The new disciplines in the social sciences include all of the following:*

- *women's studies*
- *Afro-American studies*
- *urban studies*
- *Latino-American studies*
- *international studies*
- *industrial and labor relations*
- *religious studies*

All of these disciplines occasionally utilize sociological principles, research methods, theories, and research findings.

Interdisciplinary: All of these academic fields are interdisciplinary, meaning that each approaches the scientific study of its particular interest by **combining** the **approaches** advocated by several academic disciplines.

Example: Women's studies combine the approaches of sociology, psychology, anthropology, political science, philosophy, literature, and occasionally biology, in order to derive a comprehensive understanding of what it means to be female in a particular culture.

Interactive disciplines: Each approaches the scientific study of its particular interest by *combining* the scientific approaches advocated by several academic disciplines. However, each has its own individual approach and contributes its inherent strengths and limitations.

Theme 2 SOCIOLOGICAL TERMINOLOGY: THE BASICS

*T*his theme provides explanations for most of the major words or phrases used in sociology. By understanding the meaning of these terms, used frequently hereafter, the reader will be able to understand the material in subsequent Themes in this book.

Key 8 Beliefs, attitudes, and values

OVERVIEW *Beliefs, attitudes, and values are judgments, evaluations, and ideas that underlie people's behaviors and influence the groups that people join and the things that these groups ultimately decide to do.*

Beliefs: Beliefs are personal judgments about the characteristics of a particular person or object. Certain features help define beliefs.
- They are individuals' statements of what they perceive to be fact, regardless of whether or not these statements are accurate or objective.
- Beliefs can never be wrong, because they are simply reflections of what an individual thinks is true.
- Beliefs may or may not be supported by evidence.

Attitudes: Attitudes are personal evaluations that an individual makes about a particular person or object, based on the individual's belief(s) about that person or object. Attitudes also share certain features.
- Unlike beliefs, which are what individuals **think** about people or objects, attitudes are how individuals **feel** about a person or object.
- Attitudes are personal **assessments** of how good or bad, right or wrong, or likable or unlikable a person feels toward someone or something else.
- Attitudes, like beliefs, can never be wrong, because they are based on how an individual feels.

Values: Values are indications of broad, vague, abstract **goals** that an individual or group has. They are based, at least somewhat, on beliefs and attitudes. Values also share certain features.
- They lack any specific object or reference point, which often makes them difficult to pinpoint.
- Values are reflected in the traits that people strive for, admire, and respect.
- The values of a group or culture are reflected in the traits considered worthy of respect and worth pursuing on a massive scale.

In American culture, bravery, beauty, intelligence, success, productivity, practicality, patriotism, democracy, and humanitarianism are considered positive traits and they are among the important cultural values.

Importance of beliefs, attitudes, and values: Beliefs, attitudes, and values provide an indication of how people are likely to act.

KEY EXAMPLE

If a person thinks that prostitution is a destructive influence in society (belief), and is, therefore wrong or bad (attitude) because it violates social norms of sexual restraint and marital fidelity (values), that person might be expected to oppose prostitution, and perhaps take action to try to stop it.

Key 9 Symbols

OVERVIEW *A symbol is any object, sound, color, design, or behavior that represents something other than itself. People use symbols as a shorthand form of language—an expedient way of communicating complex or time-consuming ideas in an easy, time-efficient manner.*

Characteristics of symbols: For symbols to be of use, their meanings must be understood and shared by most—if not all—members of the particular society or culture using them. Otherwise, they cannot communicate ideas efficiently and as intended.
- **Symbols are arbitrary**; they may or may not have any resemblance to the thing or idea being symbolized.
  1. The highway symbol for "no left turn" closely resembles the idea it is meant to communicate.
  2. The dove as a symbol of peace does not resemble the idea being conveyed.
- The meanings of symbols may remain **constant**, or they may **change** over time.
  1. The use of the color black to signify death or evil has been consistent over time in some cultures.
  2. The symbolic meaning of two fingers raised in a V was "victory" in the mid-1940s and "peace" in the mid-1960s.

Objects as symbols: Many objects function as symbols.
- The flag of the United States symbolizes America, Americanism, and patriotism.
- Coins, such as pennies and nickels, symbolize monetary value and purchasing power.

Sounds as symbols: Specific sounds often have symbolic meaning.
- The ring of a bell in school may signify that class is over.
- A beeping car horn may mean that the driver is impatient.

Colors as symbols: Colors often represent a great many things.
- White usually symbolizes purity and innocence (a bride's white wedding dress, for example.).
- Red is sometimes used to symbolize blood, courage, or passion.
- Green may represent jealousy (the green-eyed monster), envy ("green with envy"), "go" (a traffic light), or environmentalism.
- Pink is associated with femininity.
- Blue is associated with masculinity.

Designs as symbols: Certain designs or pictures may function as symbols.

- Television networks use individual logos to identify themselves and their programming.
- A pink triangle worn on clothing shows support for gay and lesbian rights.
- Golden arches on a fast food restaurant indicate that it is a McDonald's.
- The meowing kitten on television identifies an MTM production.

Behaviors as symbols: Behaviors can also be used in a symbolic way.

- Car headlights that are flashing on and off may signify one of several things.
  1. Another driver has neglected to turn the headlights on.
  2. There is an accident ahead, and other drivers should be alert.
  3. There is a police officer ahead trying to catch speeders.
- Waving one's hand at someone symbolizes hello or goodbye, depending upon the circumstances.
- Raising one's hand in class indicates a desire to speak.

Symbols in language: Language—both written and spoken—is also based on symbols. The characters that make up a language's alphabet are symbols, as are the combinations of characters that form words. They are symbols because they are used to represent sounds and ideas.

- Each language's alphabet has its own series of characters, which represent the sounds of the language.
- Although the characters of one alphabet may look very different from those of another, they often represent some of the same sounds.
- The combinations of characters or letters used to form words differ from language to language; the same combination in different languages often mean very different things.
  1. The combination of letters "t," "h," and "e" in English form the article "the."
  2. The same combination in French forms a word that means "tea." In each case, something is being used to represent something else, and people in various cultures understand what the symbols mean.

Key 10 Folkways

OVERVIEW *Folkways are the ordinary **conventions** or **habits** of everyday life. They are the minor, generally unimportant things that we are expected to do. They represent socially shared notions of proper behavior, and it is expected that people will abide by the actions prescribed by the folkways' dictates.*

Failure to conform: If people fail to conform to folkways, the social expectations at hand are insignificant enough that their violation is considered mostly unimportant. People who flout a folkway are not seen as immoral, and their folkway-violating actions are not illegal. Their actions are, however, going to be considered odd, and there is likely to be a response of some kind by others witnessing the violation.

KEY EXAMPLE

Imagine that it is lunchtime and you have brought your lunch with you. Rather than the usual lunchtime fare of soup and a hamburger or sandwich, you have brought cereal and a separate container of milk for your meal.

- How do you think people witnessing your lunch choice will respond?
- Do you think that they will notice that you are having something unusual for that time of day?
- Chances are good that your cereal will be noticed, and that it will generate at least one joking comment from a coworker who thinks that we should only eat cereal for breakfast. The mere fact that your choice of lunch menu generates a reaction indicates that some sort of social expectation has not been met.
- But the likelihood of the response being minor and the fact that your violation carries with it no moral undertones or legal ramifications, suggest that a **folkway** (rather than a norm, more, or law) has been broken.

Key 11 Norms

OVERVIEW *Norms are shared standards of expected social behavior. They are much like folkways, except that when a norm is broken, the consequences are more harsh.*

Guidelines for proper behavior in changing social situations: Whenever certain informal **rules** tell us what we should and should not do in a specific situation, these expectations reflect norms for certain situations. Just as circumstances differ from one another, so too do the norms that regulate people's behaviors from one situation to another. Norms give order and predictability to our lives. Without them, our everyday interactions would be chaotic, confusing, and difficult, because no one would know how to act around others or what to expect from the behavior of others.

Failure to conform: Breaking a **norm** is more significant than breaking a **folkway**. As with a violation of a folkway, violation of a norm does not usually result in a permanent stigma or any moral or legal ramifications for the violator. When a norm however, is broken, the violator can expect to receive a greater response or reproach from others observing or affected by the norm violation than one would receive from breaking a folkway. When norms are broken, responses typically include such things as smirks, laughs, ridiculing remarks, nasty comments, helpful suggestions for changing one's behavior to be more acceptable, and occasionally even threats to one's well-being.

Examples:
- Imagine what a trip to the grocery store would be like without norms.
  1. Some people would cut in front of others in the checkout line (one of our norms tells us that we should wait our turn).
  2. Other shoppers might wait their turn on line, but spend the entire time complaining bitterly about the inconvenience (another norm tells us to wait quietly until it is our time to check out).
  3. As we walk down the aisles to shop, people might grab food out of our shopping carts (a third norm tells us that once someone has made a selection from the grocery shelves, we do not touch it).

4. Without norms (and in this case, laws) to prevent such behavior, some shoppers might open a bag of their favorite candy and eat a few pieces without ever paying for the snack (still another norm tells us that we do not eat food in the grocery store until we have paid for it). By having norms, shopping becomes orderly and predictable.

- When someone gets too close to us during a conversation, we feel uncomfortable (a norm is telling us to maintain a certain personal space when we speak with others). Shouting might be an appropriate volume for speaking if the context is a party, but it would be highly inappropriate while watching a movie in a darkened theater (because norms tell us how loudly or softly we should speak). Other norms governing interaction between people tell us to face the person to whom we are speaking, to look directly at that person but not to stare, and to look only at that person's face while speaking.

Key 12 Mores

OVERVIEW *Like folkways and norms, mores (pro-nounced* more-ays) *are expectations for behavior. Mores are those social norms that people consider most important and most vital to their well-being or their most-cherished values. Unlike a violation of a folkway or norm, a violation of a more is considered serious.*

Violation of mores: At a minimum, violating a more is considered **unacceptable**; more typically, it is so unacceptable that it is considered **immoral**. And because mores form the basis for our laws, violating a more may also entail **breaking the law**.

Examples: Certain expectations for proper clothing provide useful examples of the distinctions among folkways, norms, and mores.

- Wearing matching clothing is a **folkway**. It is expected that we will coordinate our clothing according to social standards for proper attire, and that we will not wear colors or patterns that clash with one another. But if by mistake we wear clothes that do not coordinate, it is considered a relatively unimportant violation of the social expectations governing clothing.

- Wearing particular garments of clothing for certain social situations involves **norms**. For instance, it is generally considered inappropriate to wear shorts to church. Similarly, it is considered unnecessary and unusual to wear a tuxedo in a fast-food restaurant. People will take notice, make comments, and perhaps even avoid violators of these clothing-related expectations norms.

- **Mores** come into play when it comes to wearing—or not wearing—certain articles of clothing. For men to walk down an American street in July wearing no shirt is generally considered acceptable behavior. If a woman were to do this, however, she risks being arrested, or at the very least, receiving a number of stares, comments, or legal warnings. She has violated a more—an expectation for behavior that is considered so important that its violation represents a serious offense. The violation is considered serious because our culture values modesty among women and, in general, frowns upon nudity. A woman who walks topless down a street in the United States is likely to be labeled loose or immoral, thus violating the more governing proper clothing.

Key 13 Laws

OVERVIEW *Laws are our primary mechanisms of formal social control. They are those rules of behavior that have been formally enacted by some political authority, which are backed and enforced by the power of that political authority. Laws tell us specifically what we can and cannot do, and they provide a specific range of potential penalties that can be given to people who violate them.*

Laws reflect values: Whenever we have a law to regulate a particular **behavior**, that law exists because either the **culture** overall or some powerful group within the culture believes that the behavior in question is so important that conformity to it must be guaranteed to the greatest extent possible. Laws therefore reflect those values that are most important to a particular culture. Depending upon the specified range of penalties for a given law, we can also determine which values are considered more or less important and which behaviors are deemed more or less threatening than others.

Example of specificity of laws: If a man is caught stealing a candy bar, he knows that he is not going to be put to death because the law governing this behavior states that the violation of this law can result in anywhere from six months' probation to a maximum of six months in jail and a $500 fine—but not execution. However, if this man were found guilty of murder, he would expect a much more severe sentence.

Laws contrasted with folkways, norms, and mores: Folkways, norms, and mores are mechanisms of **informal social control**, things that people typically do to keep the behavior of others in check without having to resort to official rule enforcers. As informal means of social control, they lack the **specificity** of laws. Whenever possible, we try to regulate people's actions ourselves through folkways, norms, and mores, without involving the time-consuming and financially costly mechanisms of the legal system. There are times, however, when this is not possible, when the only way that certain behaviors can be prevented is through the official legal system. When this is the case, laws are enacted.

Key 14 Status

OVERVIEW *In our everyday language, the word **status** is usually used as though it were synonymous with **prestige**; the higher one's status, the greater one's prestige. Technically, though, this is not what the term means to sociologists. To a sociologist, status is the place—**any place**—that a person occupies in the social structure.*

Type of placement: Status may be **low**, **middle**, or **high**. In a culture such as ours, status is intertwined with such factors as income, occupation, education, gender, race, and a variety of other traits. The greater the number of culturally defined desirable traits one possesses, the greater the likelihood of occupying a high status position in the society.

Status is an important sociological concept for many reasons:
- **First**, it gives an indication of the things that people can and cannot do in society, because we link certain expectations for behavior to certain **status positions**. For example, it would be deemed unacceptable for the president of the United States, occupying a **high** status position, to tell dirty jokes to a group of reporters.
- **Second**, it gives an indication of how one is ordinarily treated by other members of society. A well-dressed, mannerly person who appears to occupy a high status position is likely to be treated very well—catered to or fauned over—by sales clerks in a clothing store, whereas a poorly-dressed, unkempt person, appearing to occupy a much **lower** status position, is likely to be treated less politely and more contemptuously.
- **Third**, it influences how people are treated when they violate folkways, norms, mores, or laws. Social research has repeatedly shown that people of **low** status are much more likely than their **higher**-status peers to be accused of crimes and, once accused, to be convicted.

Two basic kinds of status:
- **Ascribed status** is the type of social placement that we have as a result of certain **traits** that we possess—traits over which we have **no control**. The importance placed upon these traits by the society-at-large is entirely arbitrary, but it has a profound effect

on all people's lives. Ascribed status is based on such characteristics as sex, age, race, physical beauty, and intelligence.

For example, in its arbitrary determinations of what is valued and what is devalued, our culture has determined that higher status is awarded to people:

1. whose sex is male
2. whose age is approximately 30–39
3. whose race is Caucasian
4. who are good looking by our society's standards of beauty
5. who are intelligent.

- **Achieved status** is the type of placement in the social hierarchy that we have as a result of certain **characteristics** that we possess—characteristics over which we have **some** measure of personal control. Achieved status is based on such characteristics as education, altruism, trustworthiness, and work ethic. For example, in our culture, higher status is awarded to people who are well-educated, altruistic, trustworthy, and hard working.

  1. Most of us have a say in how much education we get.
  2. We alone determine how altruistic we are, how trustworthy we are, and how hard we work.

  Therefore, if we tend to be given a lower status position on the basis of our ascribed characteristics, all hope is not lost; through our achieved status markers, we may elevate our status somewhat.

Overall status: The placement that we occupy in the social structure—that is, our overall status—is determined on the basis of the **combination** of our **ascribed** and **achieved** status traits.

Key 15 Roles

OVERVIEW *Roles are what individuals are supposed to do in a given situation, based on their status in that situation. Our roles define our responsibilities in particular contexts.*

Multiple roles: We all occupy many roles in our everyday lives, each varying according to the situations in which we find ourselves.

- When I am involved with my students, I occupy the role of **professor**. When acting in this role, my responsibilities include such things as presenting information to students, answering their questions, evaluating their written work, meeting with them during office hours to help them learn more. But I am not always and not only a professor.
- I am also a **friend** to some people, a **son** to my parents, a **grandson** to my grandparents, a **sibling** to my brother and sisters, a **colleague** to the other professors in my department, a **customer** at the grocery store when I do my food shopping, a **protege** to my mentor.

All of these are different roles that I play, and each one has a different set of responsibilities that are unique to that particular situation.

Role as a reciprocal process: **Roles** and **role expectations** are not in a constant state of enforcement. On the contrary, we almost automatically perform our roles in ways that conform to the expectations that others have of us. Performing our roles correctly is a reciprocal process.

- I am able to assume and play the role of a **protege** when my mentor acts like a mentor to me, and vice versa.
- I am able to act like a **professor** when my students interact with me as if I were their professor, and vice versa.

By virtue of the normative expectations that we have for one another, we are able to occupy our roles and engage in behavior that is considered appropriate for people in these particular roles.

Key 16 Groups

OVERVIEW *Sociologically speaking, group is among the more complicated concepts to be considered. It is a **functional unit**—a combination of people who come together for some unified purpose, or to achieve some goal. It exists when there is something to be gained and when individual purposes can best be met by interaction with other people.*

Aspects of groups: These five points deserve attention and explanation.

- In order for a group to be said to exist, there must be a **set of people**, which may be as small as two or as large as several billion people, but must involve more than one person.
- The people in this set must **interact** with one another. They must either talk with each other or do something together, but what they discuss or do is unimportant. If this condition is not met, the people are acting as **individual** units, not as a group.
- The people interacting in this set must do so in an **orderly way**. Their involvement with one another must be somewhat patterned and predictable, and must be guided by folkways, norms, mores, and laws. Whatever their interaction is, it must continue to **link** them and **guide** them in continued interaction with one another. If this condition is not met, the people are engaged in an activity that could be described as a riot or as chaos, but not as a group.
- The people who are interacting in an orderly way must do so on the basis of **shared normative expectations**.
  1. Norms enable them to interact.
  2. Norms tell them how they can proceed with their interactions.
  3. Without shared norms, the group would be unable to remain together.
- People interacting in an orderly way on the basis of shared normative expectations are doing so on the basis of the **interrelation** of their statuses and roles. Groups are held together because people with different responsibilities and positions join forces to engage in some activity or to accomplish some goal. The group could not survive if everyone occupied the same role or the same status. (A group could not exist if it consisted only of leaders, with no followers.)

Types of groups: Groups can be either formal or informal, and either primary or secondary.

- **Formal group:** Members join together to accomplish a specific goal or engage in a specific activity. Formal groups have a shared responsibility and are task-oriented. Examples include:
  1. a company's board of directors,
  2. a presidential task force charged with studying pornography,
  3. the P.T.A.

- **Informal group:** Members join together accidentally or circumstantially. They are not usually organized nor task-oriented. They are not cohesive nor long-lasting, because they come about by coincidence. Examples include:
  1. people attending the same cocktail party.
  2. students in a classroom.
  3. people patronizing a local bar on "ladies night."

- **Primary group:** Members interact with one another over a long period of time. They come to know one another fairly intimately and interact casually with one another. Examples include:
  1. your family.
  2. a circle of friends from college.
  3. spouses.
  4. people working together in an office.

- **Secondary group:** Contrasts with a primary group on all of these dimensions. Members interact for a short or temporary time period, and often do not even recognize one another on sight or know each other's names. They interact impersonally with a rather formal quality to interactions. Examples include:
  1. lobbyists for a political cause.
  2. picketers at an abortion clinic.
  3. members of the U.S. House of Representatives.
  4. university professors in different departments.

Key 17 Institutions

OVERVIEW *In everyday parlance, institution refers either to a major organization or to a mental hospital. To a sociologist, however, an institution is a stable and widely-accepted cluster of **values, norms, statuses, roles, and groups** that develops around some **basic need in society**. As such, an institution is a complex phenomenon, much more complicated than the mere sum of its parts.*

An example of one major social institution: The **family** as a social institution represents many values, such as **cohesiveness, togetherness, unconditional love**, and **supportiveness**.
- As an institution, the family embodies such behavioral expectations (norms) as sharing toys with one's siblings, obeying one's parents' wishes, and not taking other family members' things without asking.
- The family consists of many statuses and roles, such as parents vs. offspring (status), mother vs. father (role), siblings vs. cousins (status and role).
- The family as a social unit also consists of a number of groups, such as siblings, spousal units, extended kin, grandparents.
- The basic societal needs, which the family fulfills, consist of such important tasks as childrearing, teaching basic social norms, and providing love and emotional support to its members.

Complexity: The **fulfillment** of these values, norms, statuses, roles, groups, and needs makes the family a very complex phenomenon. There is much more to a family than blood relationships or particular values or family norms. As an institution, there is a greater significance to what the family means in our lives than its component parts would lead one to believe.

Other examples of institutions:
- formal, organized **religion**
- professional **sports**
- the mass **media**
- the **educational** system
- the **government**
- the **military**

Key 18 Culture

OVERVIEW *Culture is one of the most important concepts in sociology. It is **the total way of life** experienced by a people. It is the multitude of influences that affect people's daily lives. Culture also consists of the way that individuals live their daily lives, the norms they use to guide their everyday existence and interaction patterns.*

Total way of life: Culture is the **totality of the existence** and the factors affecting that existence for a particular people. It is composed of the following factors:
- All of the **beliefs, attitudes**, and **values** that characterize a particular people's ways of thinking and feeling about their world
- All of the **folkways**
- All of the **norms**
- All of the **mores**
- All of the **laws** that regulate their ways of life
- All of the **groups** and the **institutions** that exist among these people

A shared way of life: Culture is **shared** among the culture's peoples because the values, folkways, norms, mores, laws, and institutions that are part of the culture are shared to a great extent among the members of a culture.
- Because it is **shared**, culture helps to unite people of different origins, beliefs, values, and life experiences within the culture.
- Even though no two individuals' life experiences are identical, such people's lives have more aspects **in common** with one another than they have **differences** from one another—the result of sharing a cultural background.

Comparing cultures: Culture is an important concept to sociologists because it enables them to look beyond the microlevel differences between groups.
- It enables them to talk in terms of shared experiences, norms, values, beliefs, and institutions—that is, a shared way of life among the people in one particular culture—as compared to another culture.
- It facilitates sociological understanding and sociological comparisons at the large (macro) level toward which the discipline strives to make its analyses.

Key 19 Subculture and
counterculture

OVERVIEW *Culture is a highly complex phenomenon consisting of many people, groups, and norms. Within a culture, there are always individuals or groups who, while sharing the common culture, differ from the overall culture in some fundamental way. When these people band together for mutual support and/or interaction, they form a* **subculture.** *Unlike a subculture, a* **counterculture** *arises when a cultural group differs in some fundamental way that is incompatible with the larger culture.*

Characteristics of a subculture:
- A subculture is a culture within a culture, and is therefore typically smaller than a culture.
- A subculture shares all of the same norms, beliefs, and values of the larger culture.
- Membership in a subculture does not preclude membership in the greater culture.
- Members of a subculture are indistinguishable from members of the culture except for the trait that makes them distinct from others living in the culture-at-large.

Examples of subcultures:
- Gay men, differing from the cultural mainstream in their homosexuality.
- Black Americans, differing from the mainstream in terms of their race.
- College students, differing from the mainstream in terms of daily routines, jobs, and social expectations for behavior.
- Trekkies, differing from the mainstream by virtue of their interest in *Star Trek*.
- Dead Heads, differing from the mainstream by virtue of their dedication to the Grateful Dead rock group.

Characteristics of a counterculture:
- A counterculture is **incompatible** with the larger culture in some fundamental way.
- Members of a counterculture believe that they cannot or should not compromise with the culture-at-large regarding the ideological differences that distinguish them from the larger culture.
- A counterculture opposes and attempts to change the features of the dominant culture with which it disagrees.

Examples of countercultures:
- The hippies of the 1960s.
- The Black Panthers and other followers of Malcolm X's philosophy of race relations.
- The communes of the 1960s.
- Central American Contras of the late 1980s.

Key 20 Cultural integration, cultural assimilation, acculturation, and amalgamation

OVERVIEW *Cultural integration, cultural assimilation, acculturation, and amalgamation all pertain to the degree of* **acceptance** *a particular group or subculture has achieved in the society-at-large.*

KEY DEFINITION: Cultural integration

The extent to which a particular group or subculture is included in the larger society.

- Greater cultural integration is a goal of most groups and subcultures because the more culturally integrated a group or subculture is, the more likely it is to be considered acceptable by the society-at-large.
- Cultural integration is best conceptualized as a continuum, ranging from total **integration** (acceptance by and participation in the mainstream culture) to total **alienation** (complete lack of acceptance by and participation in the mainstream culture).

Examples of cultural integration:
- Middle-class male professionals and Protestant work ethic-type people in their 30s are groups that are very well accepted in our society. Therefore, they are **high** on cultural integration.
- Lesbian separatists and intravenous drug users are groups that are not very well accepted in our society. Therefore, they are **low** on cultural integration.

KEY DEFINTION: Cultural assimilation

The process by which a group becomes a part of the dominant group.

- Whenever a new group or not-well-accepted group strives for greater acceptance, it confronts a stable, forceful, dominant culture that expects newer or unaccepted groups to conform to its standards if they are to achieve acceptance. If these groups elect to change themselves to conform, the changes that these groups undergo, along with the process of making these changes, constitute the cultural **assimilation** process.
- Usually, the changing group adopts characteristics of the larger, dominant group while simultaneously relinquishing some—if not most or all—of its own unique, less-accepted ways.
- The end result of the cultural assimilation process is to have the newer or previously unaccepted group become more accepted (that is, more culturally integrated) by the larger society.

Acculturation and **amalgamation** are two ways of undertaking the cultural assimilation process.

KEY DEFINITION: Acculturation

The specific process by which those people who wish to achieve cultural integration **give up** their "old world" ways and **adopt** the language, customs, norms, and values of the culture of which they are trying to become a part.

Example of acculturation: Upon arrival in the United States, the members of an Italian family that has recently immigrated speak no English and they are generally unfamiliar with American customs and norms. The American tendency is to expect others to abide by "our" rules and "our" customs if they are going to live in "our" country. Accordingly, if this newly arrived Italian immigrant family is going to achieve acceptance in America, they must:
- Learn to speak English
- Stop speaking Italian in the presence of other Americans
- Learn to obey American norms
- Abandon those Italian cultural norms that conflict with American cultural norms.

KEY DEFINITION: Amalgamation

The process by which several groups, all of which are simultaneously trying to gain greater acceptance in a particular culture, **join forces** to make their cultural assimilation process easier.

- When amalgamation occurs, each assimilating group looks to the successes and failures of other groups to see how they are faring in their efforts to achieve acceptance and to determine how they themselves might best proceed.
- As with acculturation, each amalgamating group sacrifices some of its own **uniqueness** in order to achieve a greater degree of cultural integration.
- In amalgamation, however, the various amalgamating groups first become more like one another, and then become more like the society-at-large.

Example of amalgamation: In the mid-19th and early 20th centuries, the American Temperance movement was composed of many small, distinctive groups working independently around the country to achieve reduced inebriety. These groups were so small, numerous, and geographically fragmented that they were only marginally successful. Toward the end of the 19th century, these groups started to band together, employing the "greater strength in numbers" ethos in their temperance campaign. In so doing, these groups lost their **individuality**, but became much more effective in pursuing their common goal. Not only did they gain greater **acceptance** in America, but they eventually amassed enough **power** to enact a constitutional amendment.

Key 21 Ethnocentrism, xenocentrism, and cultural relativism

OVERVIEW *Ethnocentrism, xenocentrism, and cultural relativity are sociological terms that describe different cultural viewpoints, from the extremes of negatively judging another culture to making a concerted effort to understand other cultures as they understand themselves.*

Ethnocentrism: The assumption that one's own way of life is the only correct way of life.
- Ethnocentrism tends to be a way of **negatively** judging other peoples and others' ways of life, including their norms, values, attitudes, beliefs, and customs.
- Ethnocentrism is a refusal to recognize that others' ways of life and others' values, beliefs, and attitudes are neither better nor worse than one's own, but merely different.
- Because it involves judgmentalism, and because its presence implies a less-than-open mind, ethnocentrism is the undoing of good sociological work.
- A sociologist who wishes to understand other cultures can only accomplish this goal by keeping an open mind, and by making a concerted effort to comprehend why some people do things differently than others and what these differences in attitudes, beliefs, and values mean to these people's lives.

Xenocentrism: The assumption that other people's ways of life or other cultures are **better** or **more desirable** than one's own.
- An example of xenocentrism is the purchase of expensive foreign products when comparable products are available domestically at better prices.
- Just as it is important for sociologists to avoid being ethnocentric, it is equally important—for the same reasons—for them to avoid being xenocentric.

Cultural relativism: A sociological perspective that recognizes that other cultures exist, that they have a right to exist, and that they have a right to their own characteristics, values, norms, and belief systems, even if these characteristics, values, norms, or belief systems are dramatically different from our own.

- Cultural relativism means that efforts are made to understand people's ways of life *as the people themselves understand them*, and that the person trying to derive this understanding makes a concerted effort to avoid using value judgments as understanding is formulated.
- Without employing a culturally relativistic perspective, sociologists can never develop the types of understandings for which the discipline constantly strives.

Key 22   Universals

OVERVIEW   *Any belief, attitude, value, characteristic behavior, norm, more, law, custom, tradition, group, or institution that is common to **all** known cultures is referred to as a **universal**, or as a **cultural universal.***

Essential to the human condition: Universals are rare, but this quality is precisely what makes them so important to sociology. Whenever we locate one, we know that we have discovered something that is essential to the human condition.

Number of universals: Research suggests that there are fewer than 100 (and perhaps no more than 60) universals.

General universal: Even among the universals, the specific form that the universal takes tends to differ from culture to culture around the world, even though the **general** universal exists everywhere.

KEY EXAMPLES

Having some sort of norms against **murder** is a universal, but what is considered murder differs dramatically around the world.

Religion appears to be another universal, but the types of religion that are seen and the specific forms of religious ritual and worship that are manifested, differ greatly from culture to culture around the world.

Providing **child care**, making social **status** differentiations, sanctioning **marriages**, making **tools**, and playing **games** are also general universals whose specific forms differ the world over.

Theme 3 SOCIOLOGICAL THEORY

*T*his theme provides a basic overview of some of the major theories used in sociology. This theme begins by addressing the questions, "What is a theory?" and "Why are theories important to sociology?" The theme concludes by examining three major social theories—functionalism, conflict theory, and symbolic interactionism—and explaining their relevance and importance to the discipline of sociology.

Key 23 What is a theory?

OVERVIEW *A theory is a **coherent set of hypothetical, conceptual,** and **pragmatic** principles forming the general frame of reference for a field of inquiry.*

Coherent: Ideas that are put together to form a theory must be **logically related** to one another, and then organized in some way that enhances the logic inherent in these ideas.
- When the ideas making up the overall theory are organized effectively, they combine in a way that makes good, rational sense to others.
- When these ideas are put together to form a theory, they are consistent with one another and are also complementary to one another.
- Without the specific, coherent way in which these ideas are linked to one another, a theory would be less understandable, comprehensive, and insightful.

Set of hypothetical, conceptional, and pragmatic principles: Theories are **multifaceted**—not simple or unidimensional.
- One of the things that makes a theory a theory is that several ideas are used.
- Another is the specific way that these notions are brought together.

Hypothetical: Theories provide precise, measurable, testable statements about one's **expectations** for behavior or about certain phenomena that will be observed.
- Hypothetical implies that we expect to see certain types of things happen under certain circumstances.
- In order to be a theory, these types of circumstances and expectations must be specifiable.

Conceptual: Theories consist of combinations of **ideas**, many of which will be rather abstract.
- Conceptual means that these ideas will combine to form something of greater significance, interest, and insight to us than any of the individual ideas themselves is capable of conveying.

Just as a car is more than the sum of its parts—pistons, tires, gears, and so forth—and, when assembled, can do things that these individual parts alone cannot do, so too is a theory more than the sum of its component ideas.

- How these ideas are merged, and what is created, suggested, and implied when they are combined, is where conceptual comes into play.

Pragmatic: Theories' principles are **practical**.
- Ideas that are brought together to form a theory are linked because of their ability to have some type of direct bearing on the world.
- While part of the purpose of developing theories is to predict and test the world around us, these predictions and tests are designed to be helpful and to have direct ramifications for the behaviors and/or social phenomena to which they pertain.

General frame of reference for a field of inquiry: Theories provide us with a basis for looking at the world around us.
- Whenever we use a theory, it provides us with some types of insights at the expense of other insights.

KEY EXAMPLE

It is difficult to be both a **functionalist** (Key 25) and a symbolic **interactionist** (Key 27) because these two theoretical paradigms make different assumptions about the social world.

- Every theory guides its followers in specific directions while simultaneously neglecting others.
- All individuals must determine whether the explanations offered by particular theories are convincing to themselves or whether other explanations should be considered.

Key 24 Why are theories important to sociologists?

OVERVIEW *Theories are important to sociologists because: (1) theories lend support and interpretability to **empirical research findings**, (2) theories expand sociologists' attention to focus on the **aggregate** level and enable them to account for large group-level **behaviors** and **phenomena**; and (3) theories can provide us with an **historical context** for understanding the social world and for predicting future events.*

Determination of causality: Sociological research can never truly **prove** anything.
- Because human beings and social phenomena are so variable and unpredictable, no rule can ever be designed to apply to **all people** or to **all examples** of a particular phenomenon.
- Therefore, when sociological research uncovers a particular finding, even when this finding is heavily supported by data, it merely **lends support** to particular conclusions.
- Researchers would be able to say that their data support a particular conclusion, which is consistent with their theories, or conversely, that the data do not appear to support the theoretical predictions being examined.

Statistical significance testing: Theories are useful in that they help give **meaning** to statistics.
- Theories help sociologists strengthen their abilities to draw conclusions from their research while at the same time providing the impetus for conducting social research in the first place.
- By developing theories **before** undertaking research, sociologists outline what they **expect** to find, the **conditions** under which they expect these findings to occur, and the **rationales** for such expectations.
- When sociologists obtain a finding that is statistically significant and consistent with their theoretical predictions, they can use that as **evidence** to support their theory.
- If social research is not theory-driven from the start, then the researcher doing the study cannot determine whether any statistically significant findings obtained are **real** or whether they

are merely **statistical artifacts** resulting from the ways that statistics are calculated.

- Some scholars liken social theories to stories, each of which is premised on its own logic, rationale, concepts, and conceptions. These stories are then sometimes subjected to verification via statistical analysis, and sometimes they are not.
- Other scholars argue that a theory has no value unless its principles can be subjected to some type of **verification**.

Macrolevel focus: Theories are of use to sociologists because they enable sociologists to employ a macrolevel (that is, large-scale, and focused on the broadest rather than the narrowest way of looking at things) focus in their work.

- Theories consist of combinations of ideas, combinations of expectations for behavior, and explanations of the circumstances under which certain behaviors or phenomena are expected to be present or absent.
- By bringing these ideas together into a coherent focus, theories force sociologists to examine social behaviors and social phenomena at the aggregate or macrolevel.
- Without such a larger-level focus, sociologists' focus would be too small (or microoriented) to accomplish the things that the discipline tries to do.

Understanding the contemporary world: Theories are useful to sociologists because they help sociologists to understand not only the world in which we live but also how our contemporary world evolved into its **present** form and how it is likely to evolve in **future** years.

Key 25 Functionalism

OVERVIEW *A functionalist approach to studying society examines how each part of society contributes to the overall **functioning** of the social system. The major underlying assumptions in functionalism are that every part of society exists because it (1) contributes something positive to the overall stability and functioning of the society, (2) serves some purposes, and/or (3) fulfills some basic needs. Conversely, anything that is not found in a particular society is absent because the society does not need it in order to exist.*

Positive contributions: Even things that most of us would consider to be harmful or detrimental to society (for example, prostitution, poverty, or racism) are viewed by functionalists as providing some **positive** (necessary) **contributions** to society.

KEY EXAMPLE:

A purely functionalist explanation of "the world's oldest profession" would claim that the reason there is prostitution in our culture is that our culture has a vested interest in the continued existence of prostitution.

- One functionalist argument might be that prostitution serves as a release of sexual energy. By hiring prostitutes, some people— particularly those who are, for whatever reasons, unable to locate suitable nonprostituting sexual partners—are able to have their sexual needs met.
- Another functionalist line of reasoning might relate to governmental interests. In some areas, there are so many prostitutes arrested that the judicial fines paid by convicted prostitutes amount to substantial revenues; therefore, there is a vested interest in sustaining it, *not* in eliminating it.
- A third line of functionalist reasoning might be job related. By allowing prostitution to continue, we allow the prostitutes to maintain a means of financial subsistence and independence that

they might not otherwise have. In addition, other people in society, such as vice-squad police officers, might be out of work if prostitution ceased to exist.

Manifest and latent functions of social phenomena: Manifest refers to those functions that are the explicit, outward, or obvious reason why we have something in society; **latent** refers to the less-obvious, more-hidden-from-view, implicit reasons why something exists in society.

Example: Why does someone elect to have a candlelight dinner?
- The manifest function of the candles is to provide illumination, to enable the couple to see one another as they dine together.
- If illumination were all that was desired, however, then incandescent or fluorescent light bulbs would serve the purpose just as well—or better—and with less inconvenience.
- Thus, if we wish to understand why someone *really* chooses candlelight at dinner, we must consider the latent functions of the candlelight, too. It symbolizes romance and creates an atmosphere, an ambiance, a mood.

KEY PERSONALITIES

Herbert Spencer: A sociologist who contributed the following ideas to the functionalist perspective: (1) Social organizations form because they help fulfill some need, and this need must be identified and understood if we wish to understand more about the organization in question. (2) Those social phenomena or behaviors that we would logically think of as being bad or dysfunctional for society are actually **practical**.

Emile Durkheim: Considered by many to be the "father of functionalism," Durkheim indicated that social phenomena occur for two reasons: (1) to fulfill some specific social void or need and (2) to help establish and maintain social order. Durkheim also believed that a full explanation of sociological phenomena would, by necessity, have to utilize **both** *historical* **and** *functional analyses.*

Thorstein Veblen: A sociologist whose primary contribution to functionalism was a distinction that he made between **manifest** functions and **latent** functions of social phenomena. He highlighted the need to look beneath the surface, not taking the obvious for granted in order to truly understand why our society sustains and continues to sustain the existence of certain behaviors and phenomena.

Key 26 Conflict theory

OVERVIEW *A conflict perspective examines systematic patterns of **benefits and deprivations**, patterned **social struggles**, and patterned **competition** within society in an effort to determine who systematically suffers and who systematically benefits from social inequalities. Conflict explanations of social behaviors and social phenomena tend to focus on power struggles, social stratification, and political involvements. Typical of conflict theory is the belief that unequal power relations in society inevitably lead to conflict, and the notion that conflict of this type is a predictable part of human social interactions.*

Conflict theory vs. functionalism: Unlike functionalism, conflict theory does not focus on social stability as an explanation of social behavior and/or social phenomena.

Competitive interactions among social groups: A conflict analysis of a particular social behavior or social phenomenon would assume that, when people interact, they almost always act so as to maneuver against one another, in an effort to gain **personal** or **social class advantages** over one another.

- Members of each social class are seen as being self-interested trying to achieve personal satisfaction and/or to minimize personal dissatisfaction.
- Conflict theory typically assumes that people **interact** with one another as members—almost as if they were representatives—of particular groups or social classes that are in some sort of competition with one another.
- Through their competitive **interactions**, these group and social class members come to understand their **status** in society, what their **needs** are, and how their own personal and class interests can best be pursued.

Material resources: A conflict analysis might also examine the material arrangements influencing particular social interactions.

- Most situations involve some type of **inequality** between interacting parties.
- A conflict analysis might assess the **resources** available to each of

the interacting parties, how evenly these resources are distributed, and how any unevenness affects them.
- The conflict analysis might strive to determine how the advantaged party tries to **dominate** the disadvantaged party and how, in turn, the disadvantaged party responds.

KEY PERSONALITIES

Karl Marx: Suggested that society is a composite of antithetical forces that generate social change by their constant **tensions** and **struggles** with one another.
- Struggle, he believed, is the essential force underlying social progress.
- "Man is a perpetually dissatisfied animal," he wrote. "When primary needs have been met, this leads to new needs."
- It was also Marx's belief that people often try to satisfy their own needs, rather than working communally toward the fulfillment of the needs of all people.
- Those people with the capital and/or the power to have their needs met will take advantage of that situation, exploiting others specifically so they can meet their own needs.
- This, Marx believed, accounted for the exploitation of labor in society; it also accounted, at least in part, for the development of social class **differentiations** in society.

C. Wright Mills: Best known for his work on "the power elite"—key people in society who, by virtue of their positions in life, are able to **control** the lives and resources of large numbers of other people.
- This power elite consists of groups of people who will do whatever it is that they must do in order to **maintain** their power or to **gain** additional power.
- To derive any meaningful understanding of society, we must begin by identifying the key power holders and understanding how they use their power, over whom they use their power, and under what circumstances they use their power.

Key 27 Symbolic interactionism

OVERVIEW *As a guiding theoretical paradigm in sociology, symbolic interactionism aims to understand people's behaviors as the people themselves understand them. Symbolic interactionists believe that all individuals bring unique interpretations of their own actions with them to **every** interaction they have. Similarly, the people with whom they interact are constantly developing their own unique interpretations of others' words and behaviors. We must therefore develop an understanding of what people's words and actions mean to **them**, as they engage in communication with other people. According to symbolic interactionists, to truly understand the group process,* each member's beliefs, attitudes, values, and behaviors must be examined and understood in their proper context.

Importance of context: Without an understanding of **context**, symbolic interactionists believe, we cannot truly comprehend the actions of a particular group.
- Symbolic interactionists contend that a purportedly objective outsider trying to explain a group's behaviors might be misled by looking merely at the group members' overt actions.
- Symbolic interactionism posits that anything that people experience or define as real is real (by virtue of those experiences or definitions).

KEY EXAMPLE

Saying "I hate you" can have very different meanings in different contexts with different interacting parties. It cannot simply be assumed that the two parties intensely dislike one another on the mere basis of the utterance of the words. Rather, it must be ascertained from the participants themselves what the words mean to them, within a particular social context. While they may indeed mean to communicate that the speaker dislikes the person to whom the words are spoken, they might also indicate envy ("You're so skinny—I hate you.")

- Only the people interacting can truly know what their interaction means; this is the type of understanding that symbolic interactionists try to achieve.

KEY PERSONALITIES

Herbert Blumer: One of the best known symbolic interactionists, whose major work on this subject was entitled *Symbolic Interactionism: Perspective and Method.* Blumer noted that:
- Human beings tend to treat social objects primarily in terms of the meanings they **attribute** to those objects rather than to these objects' intrinsic character.
- Because humans' responses and behaviors are shaped by what others **say** and **do**, these responses and behaviors cannot be accounted for by the traditional sociological variables (for example, background characteristics of the interacting parties, structural characteristics conceivably influencing their dialogue).
- Person A's responses and behaviors can only be explained and understood after one observes how Person B responds to A's initial behaviors.
- People are always engaged in a process of **interpretation, evaluation**, and **definition** of their situations.

George Herbert Mead: A noted sociologist whose significant contribution to symbolic interactionism was a distinction that he made between "I" and "me."
- "I" referred to the response of one person to the attitudes of others; it is the **self-identified** actor-as-initiator in a social interaction.
- "Me" is the organized set of attitudes that one assumes as a result of interacting with others; "me" is more passive than "I."
- As a "me," people think of themselves as objects of others' opinions, words, judgments, and/or actions; as an "I," people think of themselves as actors who can affect other people's opinions, judgments, and actions.
- Social interaction is a **reciprocal** process: How we act will determine how others will treat us; this, in turn, feeds back into how we then treat them.
- To understand the social interaction process, we must look at both how **individuals** behave and how **others** treat them.

Theme 4 SOCIAL RESEARCH
METHODS

*T*he keys in this theme are designed to explain how sociologists do research. Several of the major social research-related concepts (including random sampling, convenience sampling, bias, validity, reliability, generalizability, operationalization) are explained, as is their relevance to the performance of sociological investigations. In addition, several of the keys in this theme explain various social research methodologies and the advantages and disadvantages of employing each. The goal here is not only to help the readers understand how sociologists do their research, but also to explain to readers the kinds of research-related issues that are faced by people who wish to study human groups.

Key 28 Quantitative vs. qualitative
research designs

OVERVIEW   *Research designs in sociology can be divided into two types: quantitative and qualitative studies.* ***Quantitative*** *research designs are numbers oriented, usually involving the collection of large amounts of numerical data that will be interpreted via statistical analysis.* ***Qualitative*** *research designs are more gestalt-oriented, that is, they are designed to help the researcher develop an overall feeling and a totalistic understanding of the phenomena at hand.*

Quantitative vs. qualitative research:
- Quantitative research involves providing assessments of likelihood or probability and/or the comparisons of various groups along certain dimensions.
- When making a decision to utilize a quantitative research design, the sociologist is trying to understand the phenomena at hand by numericizing or quantifying them.
- Qualitative research rarely involves the recording and statistical analysis of *hard* (numerical) data.
- In qualitative research, the phenomena to be understood are examined directly, usually over an extended period of time, and notes are taken throughout the observation process.

KEY EXAMPLE

Suppose that a sociologist wants to study college-student drinking patterns.

- A **quantitative** approach would be to design a questionnaire including numerous questions about students' drinking habits (how often they drink, where they drink, how much they usually drink, how they feel about drinking, and so forth) and then ask a population of college students to complete the questionnaires.

- When the questionnaires are completed, the information could be transformed into numbers (for example, a value of 1 assigned to those who drink less than once a year, a value of 2 for someone who drinks a few times a year, and a value of 3 for those who drink approximately once a month), entered into a computer, and statistically analyzed.
- A **qualitative** approach to understanding college students' alcohol consumption might consist of spending a few months with college students, attending the parties and frequenting the bars where college students drink, and watching what they do in these settings.
- If a sufficient number of students were observed over a long period of time in different drinking contexts, an understanding of college students' drinking patterns could be developed.
  1. No questionnaires are ever administered in the *purely* qualitative research study, and no numbers are ever gathered. The data in such a project are the observations of the students' drinking behaviors.
  2. The interpretation of the data comes not from performing statistical comparisons, but from seeking the commonalities in the college student drinking experience across numerous students in numerous social situations.

Key 29 Using qualitative and quantitative research designs

OVERVIEW *The advantages of conducting **quantitative** research studies are (1) the availability of well-established **study designs** in the sociological literature and (2) easy, straightforward **analyses** that can be made with quantitative data. The disadvantages include (1) the absence of firsthand observations of **social behaviors** or **phenomena** and (2) problems caused by sample sizes. The advantages of **qualitative** research studies are (1) firsthand **observation** allowing the sociologist to make insights into groups, behaviors, and social phenomena and (2) **flexibility** in modifying research interests while in the field. The disadvantages of qualitative research are (1) the **subjectivity** of the researcher and (2) **uncertainty** that one is making representative conclusions.*

Advantages of quantitative research designs:
- **First**, because many books have been written about the dos and don'ts of such designs, it is relatively easy for would-be quantitative researchers to devise appropriate **study designs** and to anticipate and resolve potential **problems** and sources of **bias** that might be encountered in the actual research process.
- **Second**, data analysis is usually easy because quantitative data usually lend themselves to relatively straightforward **interpretations**.

Disadvantages of quantitative research design:
- **First**, studies that yield only numerical data lack **firsthand** observations of the social behaviors or phenomena. At times, this can make it difficult to interpret exactly what these numbers mean.
- **Second**, the quality of one's findings and the interpretations of one's statistical analyses are correlated to the sample size. A proportional difference between two groups along some dimension may be statistically significant if the sample is large, but an identical proportional difference might not yield a statistically significant difference if the sample were smaller.

Advantages of qualitative research design:
- **First**, qualitative research allows the sociologist to obtain first-hand, hands-on **insights** into groups, behaviors, and phenomena, which enables the researcher to develop a better understanding of the subject matter than is facilitated by the mere use of statistics.
- **Second**, qualitative research designs are more **flexible** and more **responsive** to the occasional need for conducting exploratory research than quantitative research designs are.

Disadvantages of qualitative research design:
- **First**, everyone interprets a situation just a little differently from everyone else: Thus, qualitative research is subject to **bias**, because it is impossible for the scholar who is doing the field observations to be 100% value-neutral.
- **Second**, qualitative research can often pose difficulties for the observer-researcher in determining just how **representative** the observations are. That is, it is almost impossible for anyone to observe enough people in enough situations over a long enough period of time to draw meaningful and representative conclusions about these people's lives.

Key 30 Social research method 1: Survey research

OVERVIEW *One of the leading quantitative social research methods involves doing **survey research**, which is based on asking specific questions that, when combined, are supposed to represent some constructs of interest to the researcher. When survey research is done, sociologists are assuming that the behavior or phenomenon that they wish to study can be analyzed and thus understood if they are given honest, thorough answers to a series of questions that relate to the behavior or phenomenon in question. There are several types of survey research: written, monitored questionnaires; mailed questionnaires; "man on the street" interviews; and telephone interviews.*

Survey research process is like a jigsaw puzzle: When sociologists do survey research, it is assumed that the behavior or phenomenon under study can be broken down into specific component parts (i.e., questions), each of which provides a piece of information that is necessary if we wish to understand the behavior or phenomenon (i.e., see the entire picture). A clear and full picture can be constructed
- if one has all of the necessary pieces of the puzzle.
- if all of the pieces are assembled properly.

Written, monitored questionnaires: This process involves having the respondents fill out a survey while the researcher or research associate proctors, to ensure that participants provide the desired information completely and correctly.
- Advantages:
  1. Improving upon the **completeness** in respondents' answers (compared to man-on-the-street interviews, for example).
  2. Ensuring that study participants **understand the questions**, because they have the ability to ask the proctor for clarification.
- Disadvantages:
  1. It is **time-intensive** because at least one research staff person must be present to monitor all respondents taking the survey.

2. It is **costly** because of the time intensiveness.
3. It is often **inconvenient** for people to arrange their schedules to come to a specific location for the purpose of taking part in a study, sometimes leading to lower participation rates.

Mailed questionnaires:
- Advantages:
    1. They offer the respondents the opportunity to complete the survey instrument at their **convenience**.
    2. It allows the researcher to assume that people who completed the questionnaire were **committed** to the project.
    3. Sociologists using this strategy assume—sometimes correctly and sometimes not—that responses to mailed questionnaires have been carefully thought out, reflecting respondents' **true responses** to the questions.
- Disadvantages:
    1. Response rates are typically low (usually well below 50 percent); introducing a potential source of **bias** into the findings.
    2. This is an **expensive** way of gathering data: Questionnaires must be printed and the costs of mailing and return postage must be assumed, in addition to the usual costs of data checking and data entry.
    3. Researchers have no way of knowing who actually **provided** the answers, even though mailed questionnaires are usually sent to specific individuals. (They may be given to a friend or another household member for completion for example.)
    4. Researchers do not know the extent to which respondents **understood** the questions, because no one is there to observe or assist them while they are filling out the surveys.

"Man on the street" interviews: In this procedure, a survey **instrument** is designed, interviewers are trained in its use (how to ask the questions, record people's answers, approach potential respondents), and then sent into the field to locate subjects who are willing to take a few moments to answer the questions.
- Advantages:
    1. Useful when a sense of **public opinion** is all that is needed.
    2. Enables the researcher to gather data fairly **quickly**, and is much **less expensive** than most other types of social research.
    3. Can often lead to interesting **insights** into people's ideas and behaviors. Some will volunteer opinions, information, thoughts, and/or insights that were not built into the survey

instrument but that may be helpful when interpreting the findings.

- Disadvantages:
  1. Obtaining a random and representative sample is very **difficult**—if not impossible—when this strategy is used, because there are few locations of which it can be claimed that the people present are typical of others in the town, state, region, or country.
  2. This technique is **intrusive:** When people are approached unexpectedly by an interviewer, they are usually otherwise involved, apprehensive about why they have been approached, and skeptical of the legitimacy of the research.
  3. People will often fail to give full or accurate answers as a result of their **distrust** of the research process.

Telephone interviews: Among the most commonly used survey research approaches, random-digit dialing is usually used to obtain access to a sample of Americans with telephones, who are called and asked survey questions.

- Advantages:
  1. **If** the topic of the study is of interest to them and **if** they understand that the interview will not take very long, most people will cooperate with this kind of research.
  2. When people do participate, the researcher can usually get a sense of whether the respondent **understands** the question and is answering **honestly**.
- Disadvantages:
  1. When called unexpectedly, people are usually a bit **skeptical** about why they are being asked to participate.
  2. People may have little **interest** in the subject of the study and may not wish to respond.
  3. They were **interrupted** while engaged in some activity, and may answer hastily or just hang up.
  4. A large number of long distance calls at the higher daytime telephone rates is usually **expensive**.
  5. Nonparticipation rates are high, as many people will hang up on an unfamiliar, unwanted caller.

Key 31   Social research method 2: Experimental research designs

OVERVIEW   *Many times, understanding a phenomenon or behavior cannot be achieved by breaking it down into a series of interrelated yet independent questions. Some phenomena and behaviors can only be understood by* **observing** *human beings* **interacting** *in their natural social contexts. When this is the case, experimental research designs may be favored.*

Two groups: Study participants are assigned at random to one of two groups, the **treatment** group (also known as the **experimental** group) and the **control** group.
- During the study, the treatment group members are placed into a specific situation set up and manipulated by the researcher, and then observed for their actions and reactions in this situation. The control group's members are left alone.
- When the experiment is completed, the two groups are compared.
  1. If the control group (which has *not* been exposed to the experimental condition) does not exhibit changes during a given time period and the experimental group does, then the changes in the experimental group will usually be attributed to the study conditions.
  2. If the control group *does* exhibit changes during the study period, these changes must be taken into account when examining the experimental group's data, so the researcher does not mistakenly attribute changes to the experimental condition when, in reality, they were due to natural or external factors that had nothing to do with the manipulations of the research project.
- Whenever experimental designs are conducted in sociology, the researcher is looking for the amount of change in the experimental group **relative to** the amount of change in the control group. The greater the **relative change**, the more the experimental condition is said to have affected people exposed to it.

KEY EXAMPLE

Assume that a sociologist wants to examine violence on television and whether it makes people more **aggressive** or **violent**. One hundred people are selected for study, preferably using some randomization strategy to ensure that the sample in representative. Fifty of these people are randomly assigned to the experimental group, the other fifty to the control group.

- The 100 subjects are given an inventory to measure their baseline levels of **aggressiveness** and **violence**.
- The typical viewing habits of the two groups are compared, making sure that the participants are comparable to one another in their ordinary television viewing habits.
- The control group is told to watch, say, four hours of television a day each day for a week, and to record the programs that have been viewed; the programs may be any that they choose.
- The experimental group is exposed to the same amount of television per day for a week, but these programs will be selected by the researcher for their greater-than-average violence content.
- At the end of the week, the two groups are again given the aggression inventory, and their scores are compared.
- If, at the end of the week, the experimental group is more violent or aggressive than the control group, the sociologist can conclude that the exposure to the programming probably caused these individuals to become more violent.
- If, however, the experimental group and the control group are **both** more violent than the week before, it cannot be concluded that exposure to the violent media messages affects people.

Key 32 Social research method 3:
Ethnographic research

OVERVIEW *Ethnographic research, often referred to as* ***participant-observation*** *research, is a type of qualitative research in which the sociologist goes into the field (the "real world") to observe people and their behaviors as they naturally occur. No questionnaires are used, and no formal questioning or interview is undertaken. No experimental condition is designed, and no intervention is performed.*

The ethnographic study process:
- Researchers must decide on the community **location** in which such a study can be done most effectively.
  1. This decision usually depends on issues such as who will be present and what social contexts there are in that community.
  2. If, for example, researchers wish to understand college student life, they must select a college or university that they believe represents all (or at least most) colleges and universities.
  3. If the study were conducted at Harvard, findings would not be representative of the student experience throughout the United States because Harvard students are not typical of all American college students.
- Ethnographers must decide how to gain **access** to the community and its members.
  1. This is a difficult aspect of the research process, because it requires that the researchers gain the trust of the people whom they wish to study.
  2. Ethnographic researchers are outsiders to practically every community that they study. They often look like outsiders in terms of their dress, grooming, or age, thus standing out from the crowd they are supposedly discreetly studying.
  3. They may also act like outsiders, because they have not become aware of the community's folkways and norms.
  4. In most communities, there are figures who can either prevent cooperation of community members or introduce important people that the researcher would not otherwise meet.

5. Such community figureheads are usually separated from the mainstream community and inaccessible to the sociologist; their input, however, is invaluable to the research process.

- Once access has been negotiated, ethnographers must **move into** the community. Numerous things take place in most communities after the standard 9:00 a.m. to 5:00 p.m. business hours.
  1. If the researcher lives outside of the community and does not see these activities, the research will not obtain a complete understanding of all facets of community life.
  2. From inside the community's boundaries, the ethnographer may walk around the neighborhood in the evening to observe the community. This increases both the community members' degree of comfort and the ethnographer's familiarity with the true happenings and workings of the community.

- Throughout the study (which typically lasts from several months to a few years), the ethnographer takes **copious notes**.
  1. These are usually written at the end of the day, every day, before the sociologist goes to sleep.
  2. At the end of the day, ethnographers are able to record their observations without being conspicuous and without interfering in their subjects' activities.
  3. By preparing notes each day, the data are more complete and ethnographers do not forget specific happenings.
  4. If an ethnographic account is to offer the insights that it is designed to provide, it will only be able to do so if the notes (that is, the data) are thorough and consistently updated.

- Prior to the formal writing stage, in which the findings are interpreted and the data are summarized in narrative form, the final step in the ethnographic research process is the ethnographer **exiting** the community.
  1. The end of the ethnographic data collection marks the end of a period of the sociologist's life.
  2. The ethnographer's role in the community's affairs during past months must be explained and goodbyes must be said.
  3. The ethnographer has been living for many months or years among the people in the community, interacting with them and befriending them. All moves require readjustments on the part of the mover, but leaving the community is essential, although it is often a difficult step.

Key 33 Social research method 4: Content research

OVERVIEW *Instead of examining human beings and their actions, sometimes sociologists wish to study a part of the tangible **human culture**. In this case, content research is often selected as the method of investigation. This type of research is most common when the focus of the research study involves some form of **mass media** (notably books, magazines, newspapers, television, film, music videos, music lyrics, advertisements).*

Most content research studies, referred to as content analyses, have two components: An **enumeration**, or quantitative, component and a **content**, or more-qualitative, component.

- In the **enumeration** stage, the sociologist tries to determine how often a specific social group, social behavior, social phenomenon, or message is being depicted.
  1. Assume that the sociologist wishes to examine violence in children's cartoons.
  2. One of the leading questions would likely be, "*What proportion of children's cartoons contain at least one violent act?*"
  3. Other important questions might be, "*How many acts of violence are shown in a typical hour's worth of children's cartoons?*" "*What proportion of the lead characters engage in at least one act of violence?*" "*Are male characters more likely than female characters to be depicted as violent?*" "*Are white characters more likely than black characters to be portrayed as violent?*"
  4. All of these questions are of the enumeration type, because they are designed to count how often a certain phenomenon is being portrayed.
- The **content** component would ask other types of questions:
  1. "*What is the nature of violence, as depicted in children's cartoons?*" "*Under what circumstances do cartoon characters engage in violent acts?*" "*What appear to be the consequences of violent acts?*"
  2. This information must be gathered in a more **qualitative** way, because it cannot simply be counted.

The content research process: When content analyses are performed:

- The researcher begins by framing research questions and then identifying some universe, or **sample frame**, of the medium to be studied (all issues of a particular magazine published between 1980 and 1989, for example).
- A **random sample** must be located and obtained from the sample frame.
- The measures to be used in the content analysis must be operationalized so that each social group, social behavior, social phenomenon, and message can be studied.
- This is done by developing a **coding book** (a content analyst's user's manual) detailing everything that will be sought, how these occurrences are to be recognized, and how the data are to be recorded and coded.
- Typically, coding books are **pretested** prior to implementation, just as questionnaires are pretested prior to use in actual survey research work.
- When the coding book has been completed and pretested, the sample items are **examined** and the data recorded.
- The final step is **statistical analysis**.

Key 34 Single-methodology vs.
multiple-methodology studies

OVERVIEW *A current trend in sociological research is to conduct studies that **combine** research methodologies, so the strengths of one can compensate for the inherent weaknesses in the other. Often, the combination sought is one that blends a **qualitative** research design with a **quantitative** approach to data collection. The intent of such complex, multifaceted research is to gather data that facilitate a genuine understanding of the phenomenon at hand (via qualitative analysis), while simultaneously providing the statistical evidence to buttress the significance of the relationships obtained (via quantitative analysis).*

Advantages of multiple-methodology studies: When it is feasible to conduct them, this is the optimal way of doing sociological research.
- The participant-observation, hands-on nature of the qualitative part of the study lends itself to developing an **insider's understanding** of the subject matter being investigated.
- The quantitative data are able to provide additional, **statistical support** for the suppositions made on the basis of qualitative analysis.

Disadvantages of multiple-methodology studies: There are three main problems with doing multiple-methodology studies:
- They are more **time-consuming** and more **time-intensive** than single-methodology studies, because data must be collected in more than one way.
- Accordingly, they are more **expensive** than single-methodology studies.
- They are much more **complicated** to perform. With a single-methodology study, only one set of logistical details must be resolved, but in a multiple-methodology study where more than one means of data collection is being used, the logistical details must be handled for both research strategies employed.

Key 35 Cross-sectional vs.
longitudinal research designs

OVERVIEW *In a **cross-sectional** research design, a group of people is examined once. This type of research is best suited to investigating relationships that are not thought to change over time or to vary as a function of age or, alternatively, where changes over time are not of interest or concern to the researcher. In a **longitudinal** study, a group of people is examined over an extended period of time, often many years. This type of research is well suited to studying how behaviors, attitudes, or phenomena change over time or how they change as a function of age.*

Advantages of cross-sectional studies: They require much less **time, money**, and **effort** to conduct.

Disadvantage of cross-sectional studies: The effects of the aging and maturation processes cannot be studied in any meaningful way.

KEY EXAMPLE

In a cross-sectional study, researchers discover that there is an **inverse** relationship between age and alcohol consumption, but they do not know how to interpret this finding.

- It may be due to an age-related effect—as people grow older, they may become less likely to drink, or they might drink less often, or perhaps they simply reduce the amount of alcohol they ingest whenever they do drink.
- The inverse association may also be due to a **cohort effect**, that is, due to differences in the drinking-related attitudes and norms with which people from different historical periods were raised. Thus, we would find a decline in alcohol use with advancing age and this relationship would have nothing to do with the aging process, *per se*.

- Cross-sectional data do not enable researchers to determine which of the preceding interpretations is correct.

Advantage of longitudinal studies: They enable the researcher to examine how things **change** over a certain time period.

Disadvantages of longitudinal studies:
- Examining people over a long period of time significantly increases the financial **costs** of doing research.
- The researcher must wait for a long **time** before data analysis can be conducted to address the initial research questions. This is often undesirable and/or impractical.
- Such studies often suffer from high **attrition rates**—loss of subjects over time.
    1. If many people are not followed and reinterviewed throughout the entire study period, serious problems of bias may occur because it is likely that the people who are lost during follow-up are systematically different from those who were available for and cooperative with the entire research study.
    2. Researchers are unable to examine the true nature of changes over time if they are unable to examine how all (or at the very least, most) study participants changed over time.
    3. Longitudinal research requires the researcher to find ways to keep track of participants' whereabouts over long periods of time; the researcher must also find ways to keep participants interested in and willing to continue their participation in the study at hand.

Key 36 Random sampling

OVERVIEW *From a methodological point of view, random sampling is the preferred way of doing sociological research. Sociologists try to utilize random sampling because it enables them to generalize their findings to larger groups; when findings are based on a random sample of some population, sociologists are able to extrapolate the findings of their **sample** of this population to the **entire** population.*

Complicated mathematical formulae: Equations have been devised to determine the specific value of utilizing random samples.
- These equations have shown that by studying as few as 1,500 people who are randomly selected from the population, sociologists can legitimately make claims that their findings represent thousands, perhaps even millions, of others.

To obtain a random sample: The researcher obtains a master list of all people or all phenomena in a particular category.
- People are selected from this master list in some systematic way, so that each person has an equal chance of being asked to participate.
- If all of the invited participants accept the offer to be included in the study (which is usually a false assumption to make), information is collected according to the predetermined research plan.

KEY EXAMPLE

If we wished to examine American adults' attitudes toward AIDS, we would look for a way to give all American adults an equal chance of being included in the sample. This is usually done by a process called **random digit dialing**, whereby a computer-generated list of random numbers is used for dialing telephone numbers all over the country.

- Researchers often test the actual randomness of their sample by selecting several variables (sex, age, and race, for instance) and comparing the demographic composition of their sample to the demographic composition of the master list, which sociologists call the **universe**, to make sure that the people sampled do resemble the people who were not selected for study. (NOTE: If *all* people have an equal chance of being selected for the study, it is possible, although unlikely, that all would be, say, age 25; if such an unlikely event occurred, the sample would not be representative. It is therefore incumbent on the researcher to test these variables.)

Key 37 Convenience sampling

OVERVIEW *As the term implies, convenience samples are based on whatever **people** or **phenomena** the researcher has available for study. Unlike a random sample, in which everyone has an equal chance of being studied, in a convenience sample, certain people have a greater chance than others to be studied.*

Example: A sociologist wishes to learn more about adults' smoking patterns.
- Instead of obtaining a random sample of adults, perhaps the sociologist only contacts adults living in a particular neighborhood, and asks them to participate in the study.
- This method is used in lieu of a random sample because people are easier to locate and probably more willing to join their neighbors in cooperating with the sociologist conducting the research.

Advantages:
- Convenience samples are easier to obtain than random samples.
- They are an expedient means of conducting research, because the researcher has a captive population that is easily located for investigation.
- They are usually less expensive than studies based on random sampling.

Disadvantages:
- Convenience sampling almost always introduces a source of **bias** into the research design when it is used, and bias is very likely to alter the results.
- Only rarely are convenience samples representative of any larger group; this makes it difficult to **generalize** the findings.
- In the above example, the chances are very high that the people living in this neighborhood do not represent all adults living in neighborhoods throughout the United States. Thus, the sociologist is limited in what can be concluded on the basis of the study.

Key 38   Research bias

OVERVIEW   *Bias refers to problems with the representativeness and generalizability of the research study, such that whatever findings are obtained are rendered questionable because of **methodological shortcomings** in the study. Bias is the undoing of good sociological research. It is impossible for sociologists to do work that is 100 percent free of bias, but the goal in conducting research is to minimize bias as much as possible.*

Ways in which bias can enter into a sociological study:
- One source of bias, referred to as **refusal** bias, **selection** bias, or **nonparticipation** bias, comes from people who are selected for participation in a particular study, but who choose not to participate for various reasons.

KEY EXAMPLE

Suppose that we wished to study American adults' drinking patterns, but only 50 percent of the people who were invited to participate in our study consented to do so.

1. Can we correctly assume that the other 50 percent of the potential respondents are similar to the people who agreed to take part in our study? Probably not.
2. Research that has been done in this area indicates that the nonparticipants in drinking studies are likelier than participants to be frequent drinkers, heavy drinkers, and problem drinkers. Thus, the 50 percent nonparticipation rate is likely to alter (bias) this study's findings.
3. Whenever nonparticipation occurs, the researcher must make a concerted effort to compare the people who did not take part in the study to those who were included in the sample.
4. As long as these two groups do not differ in any systematic way (in terms of gender breakdown, racial composition, average age, etc.), the researcher is reassured that refusal bias is kept to a minimum.

5. This problem cannot be eliminated altogether, for the question will always remain, "Is there any way in which the nonparticipants' refusal to participate in this study affected the study's results?"

- Another type of bias is referred to as **nonlocation bias**, which refers to the researcher's inability to locate certain people or items on his or her sample list.

KEY EXAMPLE

Let's assume that a telephone survey is being conducted: A working number has been dialed, but nobody answers.

---

1. Can we automatically assume that there is no difference between people who are home when the interviewers call and those who are not home when the researchers call? The answer is no.
2. Unlocated respondents may be involved in more social activities than participants who were at home at the time of the call.
3. Depending upon the kind of research being done, this difference could be very important, and could very well bias the study's findings.

- Another type of bias affecting some social research is **recall** bias, in which people's memories are relied upon.
  1. Are their memories always good? Are they always accurate and complete? The answer to these questions is no.
  2. On some subjects, people's memories are notoriously bad.
  3. If we put too much emphasis upon what people remember, we are allowing a source of bias into our study.

- It is important to note that these are but a few of the many types and sources of bias that exist, and that all forms of bias have the potential of undermining the quality of the social research studies in which they occur.

Key 39 Validity, reliability, and generalizability

OVERVIEW *Validity refers to how well we are able to measure the social behavior or social phenomenon that we have set out to measure in the manner in which we have chosen to measure it.* ***Reliability*** *refers to the reproduceability of one's findings.* ***Generalizability*** *is the extent to which a study's findings can be said to reflect the greater society or some other large social group or entity.*

Validity: The more valid sociologists' measures are, the more credence we can give to their findings.
- The researcher's goal is to develop measures that are sensitive enough to capture whatever information there is to be gotten, in a way that is both substantively accurate and thorough.

KEY EXAMPLE

Suppose that we wished to study the relationship between intelligence and success at work.

---

1. We must begin by developing a **construct**, that is, a specific way to measure the concept, that will enable us to measure intelligence.
2. We could use people's school grades as measures of intelligence, with the assumption being that people with better grades are more intelligent than those with poorer grades.
3. But is this necessarily true? No, because many intelligent people do poorly in a particular class, for a variety of reasons (such as not getting along with an instructor, personal problems).
4. Thus, the validity of using grades as a measure of intelligence would be rather low.
5. A better measure of intelligence (a measure with greater validity) is needed if the aforementioned study is to be performed successfully.

Reliability: If one has conducted **research** that gets at the true nature of the subject being examined, it would not matter when the study was conducted, by whom or where.

- The phenomenon or behavior under study does not change as a function of the sociologist's research **methodology**, although different findings could very well be obtained by using different research methodologies or measures.
- As long as research studies are done properly (as long as they are reliable), their results can be replicated.
- These studies' measures and methods must be carefully chosen prior to implementation.

KEY EXAMPLE

Consider the evaluation of your work in college, specifically a paper for an Introduction to Sociology course.

---

1. Theoretically, the paper should receive the same grade from each professor who reads it, because the actual work constituting the paper does not change.
2. If, indeed, this were the case, we could say that grading papers is a reliable method of measuring students' learning and performance in their college courses.
3. Different professors, however, are likely to award different grades to the same paper because they adhere to different grading policies or because they have different standards or expectations.
4. Thus, even though your paper's content remains the same, the grades it receives might differ.
5. Grading, then, is a measure that is low in reliability, because the same results cannot consistently be obtained in similar circumstances.

Generalizability: The ability to extrapolate one's research findings to the larger social world is the ultimate goal of sociology as an academic discipline.

- Not all research can be said to apply to the real world.
- Sometimes sociological research findings cannot even be said to apply to a population other than the specific population studied.

Sociologists A and B wish to study Americans' attitudes toward the elderly. In Study A, sociologist A obtains a sample of 100 college students enrolled in her Aging and Society course, and gives them a questionnaire inquiring about their attitudes toward older adults. In Study B, sociologist B conducts a random telephone survey of 1,500 Americans, and asks them about their views concerning the elderly.

1. Which of these studies is more likely to come up with results that truly reflect American society's attitudes toward old age?
2. The answer is Study B, because it is based on more people who were randomly sampled, as opposed to Study A, whose respondents are younger, better educated, and more attuned to issues relevant to the elderly than the average American.
3. Thus, sociologist B would be more able than sociologist A to generalize her findings to the larger society, to claim that her findings reflect all Americans' attitudes toward the elderly.

Key 40 Operationalization

OVERVIEW *Whenever social research is done, every concept that will be examined must be measured in some way. **Operationalization** refers to the specific definition that is given for a term or the specific manner in which a concept is to be measured in a particular research study. Most concepts can be measured in a variety of ways, and the specific manner in which a concept is measured can alter a study's findings considerably. Consequently, operationalization is the process that determines what exactly a study's variables mean. By operationalizing variables, a sociologist enables other researchers to evaluate a particular study's findings—to know exactly what was done and how it was measured.*

Example: Consider the following example from this writer's research on college students' drinking patterns:

- One of many things examined was the status of alcohol use among the students in the sample—that is, whether each student was an abstainer from or a consumer of alcoholic beverages.
- In the survey instrument used for this study, three separate measures could be used to assess drinking status:
  1. "Do you ever drink alcoholic beverages of any kind?"
  2. The students' usual frequency of drinking and their usual amount of consumption per drinking occasion were combined into a single variable measuring typical monthly alcohol consumption.
  3. Students were asked to label themselves as either a drinker or a nondrinker, for the purpose of answering a separate series of questions.
- The results were interesting: 95.1 percent of the students were labeled as drinkers on the basis of the first method of assessment, compared to 94.9 percent for the second method, and 74.7 percent for the third.

- Any conclusions drawn about the proportion of students who are drinkers would differ depending upon how the term drinker was defined. Thus, the operationalization of the term *drinker* was very important to the research.
- Sociologists must always consider how the definitions of their concepts are likely to affect their results.

Key 41 Hypothesis testing and statistical significance

OVERVIEW *Human behavior is **varied** and **unpredictable**. As a result, one of the problems inherent in doing social science research is that for every rule there are numerous exceptions. Therefore, it is important to recognize that sociologists' studies never prove anything. Their findings can lend support to a particular notion, or they can fail to find support for a particular relationship; but because people rarely operate in an "if X then Y" fashion, social research can never anticipate precisely what will happen.*

Hypothesis testing: The **goal** of sociological research is to advance knowledge by discovering evidence in support of or in opposition to certain hypothesized relationships.

- Sociologists begin their research process by formulating **hypotheses**, which are specific, testable statements of expected relationships.
- These expectations are based on a combination of the theoretical **orientation** of the sociologist and previous **research findings** in a particular subject area.
- Once generated, hypotheses are used to guide the research process.
- It is crucial that sociologists begin the research process by formulating hypotheses, because only then will they have a strong conceptual backdrop against which to interpret data.
- Without such a backdrop, they are subject to the difficulties in interpretation posed by reliance upon statistics.
- When social research is theory-driven, it is easier for the sociologist to account for findings and to put them into a meaningful context.

Statistical testing: How certain must we be that our findings did not occur merely as a result of chance before we will accept them as real or as meaningful?

- For sociologists, the **minimum level** of statistical assuredness that is required before any finding will be considered significant (that is, reflective of a true relationship between variables) is 95 percent.

- If, when a statistical computation has been completed, the sociologist determines that a particular finding would be reliable 94.99 percent of the time, it does not meet the minimum level because it is less than 95 percent.
- Typically, such a finding would be discarded as nonsignificant, indicating a lack of support for a relationship between the variables under study.
- Sociologists set their standards high, refusing to accept the value of anything that could occur by chance more than 1 time in 20. This criterion is used in the social sciences to strengthen people's confidence in social research findings.

Key 42 Type I and type II errors

OVERVIEW *Two major problems can arise in the use of statistical significance testing in sociological research: Type I and type II errors. Type I error involves a **false positive**, a finding that is reported as being statistically significant when, in reality, it is meaningless (not truly reflective of a relationship between two variables) and should not have occurred. Type II error refers to a **false negative**, failure to find a significant relationship when, in reality, there is one in existence.*

Example of type I error: Imagine that you had a blood test to determine if you are pregnant.

- You have abstained from sexual intercourse of all kinds for the past year, but somehow, your test results come back positive, telling you that you are pregnant.
- This is a Type I error, the result of using a measurement construct that is so sensitive that it inadvertently picks up on things that are not really there.
- Remember that the convention in sociology to rely upon a minimum confidence level of 95 percent before labeling a finding as statistically significant still leaves room for one error in every 20 calculations. While this error rate is small, it is, nevertheless, present.

Example of type II error: Imagine that you were pregnant and went to a doctor for a test to confirm your suspicion.

- The test results come back negative, suggesting that you are not pregnant, but all the while, a fetus is growing inside you.
- This is a Type II error; the test has failed to discover a real occurrence (your pregnancy).
- In social research, Type II error is usually the result of constructing measures that are not sensitive enough, or using constructs that are inadequate to measure the behavior or phenomenon that they are supposed to measure.

Both types of errors: An important point is highlighted: sociological research data are only as good as the measures that yielded them in the first place.

Theme 5 SOCIALIZATION

*T*his theme addresses the concept of socialization, or the process by which we come to learn about the social world and how to be human social beings. The theme begins by explaining what socialization means, and then proceeds to explain the roles that both nature and nurture play in the human socialization process. From there the theme addresses the concepts of successful versus unsuccessful socialization, the different types of socialization, and the agents of socialization. Together, the keys comprising this theme provide an understanding of how human beings develop from animal beings to human social beings.

Key 43 What is socialization?

OVERVIEW   *Socialization is the process by which humans learn how to become and act human. It is how we become transformed from merely living **animal** beings to human **social** beings, capable of living and functioning in human societies. It is the process by which individuals learn to act in groups (in their families, with their peers, or at work, for example). It is via the process of socialization that people are able to become and to remain as participating members of a human society.*

Learned behaviors: We **learn** our folkways, norms, mores, and laws.
- In order to become a member of human society, we must learn what is expected of us and how we are allowed/expected to act in specific situations.
- Almost without exception, whenever someone does, thinks, or feels something, that behavior, thought, or emotion had to be learned, implying that at some time, it must have been taught to the individual.
- Thus, all of these things are **socialized**.

Emotions: Most of our emotions are socialized. We are taught what emotions to feel, and the circumstances under which we are and are not allowed to experience them.

KEY EXAMPLES

- Feeling jealous because someone is paying inappropriate attention to one's boyfriend or girlfriend
- Being envious of a coworker's promotion
- Becoming angry when someone cuts in front of you in line

All of these feelings are **learned**.

Thinking: Socialization processes also teach us what to think.

KEY EXAMPLES

- Believing that there is one God
- Believing that men are better than women at certain things (and vice-versa)
- Believing that older people are set in their ways
- Believing that people should constantly work harder to earn more money

All of these beliefs are **learned**.

Values: Our values are also socialized.

KEY EXAMPLE

If one believes that patriotism, bravery, altruism, and beauty are worth striving for, it is important to recognize that we are **socialized** into having these values.

Personal morals: All of our own personal moral codes are also socialized.

KEY EXAMPLE

Considering rape, adultery, immaturity, and lying to be wrong are learned morals; they are not innate.

Adjustment to new situations: Socialization is also important in that it is the learning process that teaches us how to act in new and unfamiliar situations.

KEY EXAMPLE

When you first began college and were not sure what was expected of you socially and academically, you learned, probably by trial and error, how to act and how to get along.

1. You may have learned by talking to or observing upperclass students who were more advanced in college than you were at the time.
2. Another part of learning may have occurred by getting into trouble academically or by committing some sort of violation in your residence hall.
3. As you progressed through college, you began to learn how college works, that is, you became **socialized**.

Ongoing process: The process of socialization never totally stops: As long as people continue to interact with other people, they continue to rely upon socialization to teach them how to do so effectively. For most people, socialization is a lifelong process.

Key 44 Nature vs. nurture in socialization

OVERVIEW *Nature refers to traits with which we are born; nurture refers to those traits that must be taught. When it comes to our socialization experiences, both nature and nurture are important and relevant to understanding what we do, think, and feel.*

Nature sets the stage for the pathway that nurture takes: The socialization process begins with nature—with those skills and abilities that one possesses from the start—and progresses according to how these skills and abilities are perceived and responded to by others in one's life.
- Early in their lives, most people demonstrate some abilities that set them apart from others their age.
- For some, it may be athletic ability.
- For others, it may be a demonstrated capability of meeting and getting along with other people.
- For still others, this ability may be a manifestation of creativity, such as painting or drawing or writing.
- As long as the innate ability is a positive (desired, valued) trait, it is likely to be supported (**nurtured**) by others in one's life.

Relative importance of nature and nurture: Neither nature nor nurture is more important than the other; both are important.
- Without nature's contribution, we would not possess the abilities or skills that we are encouraged to develop and integrate into our lives.
- If the socialization process did not contribute the nurture part, many of these skills and abilities would never be fully utilized.

Progression of nature to nurture: When the skills and abilities that have been provided by nature become evident to others, these individuals tend to pick up where nature left off, and thus the nurture process begins. Nature sets the stage for the pathway that nurture takes.

Concern of sociologists: While both nature and nurture are important components of the behavioral process, both parts are not of equal interest to sociologists.

- Nature is typically of less interest to sociologists than nurture because nature is inbred, while nurture is socialized.
- Key aspects of the socialization process of interest to sociologists are:
  1. exactly which skills and abilities are nurtured once they become manifest.
  2. why our culture tells us to nurture these particular skills and abilities and not others.
  3. how these skills and abilities are encouraged and developed.
  4. what effect that encouragement and development has on the person possessing the skill or ability and the people affected by that individual.

Key 45 Successful vs. unsuccessful
socialization

OVERVIEW *Successful socialization is said to have occurred whenever the behavior, belief, attitude, or norm that our culture or particular individuals in our society is trying to teach or instill in us actually becomes a part of our behavioral repertoire, belief structure, or attitude structure. Whenever someone tries to teach us something or tries to instill a particular belief, attitude, value, or norm into us and it is not learned, a process of **unsuccessful** socialization is said to have occurred.*

Successful socialization: The process of successful socialization is also referred to as **internalization**.
- When socialization is successful, people are changed. They possess something new—some new behavior, belief, attitude, or value—something that did not characterize them or their actions before the socialization process began.
- Whenever sociologists discuss something having been socialized, they are referring to this successful socialization, or internalization, process.

Unsuccessful socialization: When the person who is supposed to have learned the new behavior, belief, or attitude remains unchanged, unsuccessful socialization has occurred.
- The behavior or attitude does not become a part of one's behavioral repertoire, belief structure, or attitude structure.
- Unsuccessful socialization is usually the result of one (or more) of four things.
  1. The socialization may not succeed because the agent of socialization (Key 47) is not adept enough at teaching the behavior, belief, attitude, or norm to the person in question.
  2. Unsuccessful socialization may occur because the person to be socialized is not receptive to the behavior, belief, or attitude that he or she is expected to learn.

KEY EXAMPLE

You are not a racist but your neighbors are, and they want you to become a racist, too. They talk to you frequently, trying to convince you that you should change your views of people of different races to match theirs. If you still disagree with them, and if their logic simply does not persuade you, you will probably remain a nonracist. Your neighbors' efforts to socialize you to become a racist have failed.

3. Socialization may be unsuccessful because there is a poor fit between the person to be socialized and the behavior, norm, or attitude to be learned.

KEY EXAMPLE

A clumsy boy wants to learn how to play baseball, and his father—himself a good baseball player—wants to teach his son how to play. So they practice. The father shows his son how to hold the bat, how to stand at the plate, and how to swing—but to no avail. After many lessons and much patience from the father, and despite his motivation to learn how to be a better ball player, the boy is still poor at baseball, and the father's socialization efforts have not been successful.

4. Socialization might also be unsuccessful because the individual receives conflicting and contradictory messages from different agents of socialization.

KEY EXAMPLE

Julia's primary agents of socialization are her family members, friends, teachers, and television, and the phenomenon to be socialized relates to the treatment of people based on their physical appearance. Julia's parents and teachers tell her that "a book cannot be judged by its cover," that "beauty is only skin deep," and that she should not decide whether she likes people based on their looks. But Julia's friends and some television programs convey a different message: Looks matter a great deal, and "anybody who is anybody" wants to be seen with a good-looking person. Which agents of socialization will Julia end up obeying? There is no way to know the answer for certain, because Julia may be socialized successfully by the former, the latter, or by neither group.

The following Key Figure presents a visual depiction of the socialization process that Julia undergoes in this example.

KEY FIGURE

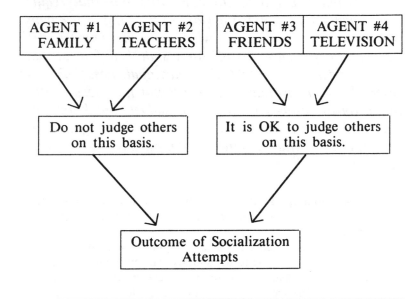

Key 46 Five types of socialization

OVERVIEW *Primary socialization takes place early in life, as the human being gradually learns to become a social being. Anticipatory socialization is the type of learning that helps prepare people for future roles. Developmental socialization (sometimes referred to as secondary socialization or adult socialization) is the process by which people take the skills, norms, behaviors, and values that they have already learned and apply them to new situations that require adjustments to their existing ways of thinking or behaving. Reverse socialization occurs when someone younger, with less world experience, instills some skill, belief, or attitude into an older, more world-wise individual. Resocialization resembles both primary and developmental socialization but involves some sort of sharp, sudden break in one's surroundings or culture, and necessitates learning a new set of behaviors, attitudes, beliefs, and norms, in order to thrive socially.*

Primary socialization: Think of the difference between how little a three-week-old infant knows and how much more a three-year-old child knows.
- People develop language skills, beginning with how to make sounds, then learning to use sounds that represent specific ideas (words), then learning to combine these words to convey more complex ideas (sentences), then learning the proper ways to use language (grammar, spelling, syntax).
- People also learn basic cultural norms—the dos and don'ts of living in their social world—and basic beliefs, attitudes, and values.
- Primary socialization is the process by which *all* of these skills (and countless others) are acquired, mastered, and internalized.

Anticipatory socialization: This type often involves various types of role playing, whereby young people usually learn how they are expected to behave based on other people's reactions to their playtime role-playing.

- When children of different families play house, some adopt the role of mommy while others play daddy.
- By play-acting while playing house, they learn what sorts of things they might be expected to do when they get older—when they become mommies or daddies.
- By interacting with the other children, they learn that "My daddy doesn't do this" or "Mommies always do that."
- They learn (via interaction and **socialization**) how to **anticipate** how they should behave when, later in life, they become parents.

Developmental socialization:
- New ways of acting or thinking are required of the individual.
- If, during a lifetime, someone fails to develop new beliefs, attitudes, or behaviors, that person would have difficulties getting by in new situations because they are more complex, or merely different in some way, than previously encountered contexts.
- By engaging in a process of trial and error, the person in this new, unfamiliar situation makes gradual adjustments in thinking, feeling, or behaving in an effort to fit in better.
- Thus, in an effort to fit in better, the person in this new, unfamiliar situation makes gradual adjustments in thinking, feeling, or behaving, by engaging in a process of trial and error.
- Thus, the person develops certain traits for the new situation, and learns how to incorporate them into a belief structure, attitude structure, and behavioral repertoire.

Reverse socialization: This circumstance occurs when an older person (who is presumably more experienced and knowledgeable) learns from a younger person (who is presumably less experienced in the world).

- When a young girl learns to use a personal computer in school, and then shows her parents how to operate their at home computer, the girl is engaging in a process of **reverse socialization** with her parents.

- When a first-year university faculty member possessing good statistical skills explains to one of his more-senior colleagues how to perform certain complex statistical analyses, the learning process taking place for the senior colleague involves **reverse socialization**.

Resocialization: The individual who is to be resocialized is abruptly taken out of a familiar culture or surroundings, and is placed in a completely different, alien situation where new behaviors, beliefs, attitudes, and norms must be learned and adopted, in order for the person to survive socially.

KEY EXAMPLES

- Incarceration in a maximum-security prison. That individual would have to become resocialized into the prison subculture, because many different norms exist in prison than in society-at-large (for example, unlike society at large, people in prison are not socialized to think of police officers as being there to support, help, or be of service to them).
- Joining the military. This involves an entirely different way of life than civilian living does.
- Moving from an ordinary residence to a convent or monastery. This is a situation in which resocialization must occur, because someone's prior socialization experiences are inadequate as guidelines of how to live and survive in a new environment.

Key 47 Agents of socialization

OVERVIEW *Sociologists refer to any person or institution that participates in an ongoing capacity in people's socialization process as an **agent of socialization**. Anybody or anything that teaches people about beliefs, attitudes, values, norms, or behaviors is acting as an agent of socialization, but sociologists usually reserve the use of this term for those persons or institutions who provide such learning (1) frequently, (2) for large numbers of people, or (3) on an ongoing basis.*

Four important agents of socialization: Although there are many agents of socialization in our society at any given time, four are particularly important: the **family**, one's **peers**, the **educational system**, and the **mass media**.

The family: Averaging cultures throughout the world, the family is probably the **single most important agent** of socialization.
  - The task of primary socialization is almost the exclusive responsibility of the family, including teaching our basic behavioral dos and don'ts or social norms, our feelings and emotions, and our values, among other things.
  - Consider how much we learn from our parents, grandparents, aunts, uncles, and siblings about what to do, what not to do, what to think, what not to think.
  - The potency of the family as an agent of socialization is also bolstered the fact that the family is the only socializing agent that will be with us throughout our entire lifetimes.

Peers: This group is primarily responsible for **anticipatory** and **developmental** socialization.
  - By interacting with others of our own age and status, we learn what is expected of us, how to fit in with society, and how to attain others' acceptance.
  - We learn how to adjust to new situations as a result of our interactions with other people who are already in these situations.
  - Our peers are among our most influential agents of socialization from childhood onward in our lives, especially during the childhood and adolescent periods.

Educational system: This institution instills a great many **beliefs**, **attitudes**, and **behavior** that no other agents of socialization teach us.

- It provides people with knowledge about a variety of subjects in various classes in school.
- It teaches about the importance of punctuality, patriotism, learning to dress appropriately, developing patience and respect for our peers (raising our hands to speak, waiting our turn to speak while someone else is talking, for example), and accepting and respecting the authority of people who are not our relatives (who may be teachers, hall monitors, professors, advisors, principals, or guidance counselors).

Mass media: The media are among our most potent sources for providing and reinforcing **anticipatory** socialization.

- Through our exposure to books, magazines, television programs, radio shows, films, newspapers, and the other media forms, we are literally bombarded with messages about every group and every behavior and every belief imaginable.
- When the mass media provide consistent portrayals of certain groups, and when we are exposed over and over again to these messages, we become susceptible to believing what we see, read, and hear.

Theme 6 GENDER STUDIES

*T*he purpose of this theme is to introduce the reader to the main sociological issues involved in being male or female in our culture. The first key in this theme explains the difference between the terms "sex" and "gender." Most of the remaining keys address the issue of how people come to think of themselves as being male or masculine beings, or as female or feminine beings. These definitions of oneself are, to a great extent, shaped and reinforced by the people who raise us and the people with whom we interact in our daily lives. The last three keys in this theme focus on how our gender identities are initially created and, subsequently, how they undergo a continuous refinement process throughout our lifetimes.

Key 48 Sex vs. gender

OVERVIEW *The terms* **sex** *and* **gender** *have different meanings. Sex refers specifically to one's internal and external sexual organs. There is no social or cultural component to sex. Gender, on the other hand, is the personal, social, or cultural assignment of being male or female.*

Sex: A purely physical determination of whether one is male or female.
- If one has a penis and testicles, then that individual's sex is male; if the person has a vagina, Fallopian tubes, and ovaries, then that individual's sex is female.
- Personal perception and one's self-identity do not factor into the determination of one's sex.
- The only exception to a person's sex being male or female is seen in people known as **hermaphrodites**, individuals with a relatively rare type of birth defect that leaves them with the sexual organs of both males and females.
  1. A hermaphrodite might have a penis and a vagina, or a penis and ovaries, or any other combination of the male and female sexual organs.
  2. Classification of a hermaphrodite's sex is made on the basis of the sex chromosomes: If the person's chromosomes are XX, the hermaphrodite's sex is considered female; if the person's chromosomes are XY, the sex is considered male.

Gender: Unlike sex, which is based exclusively on one's sexual organs, gender is based on a series of labels that people apply to themselves and that others place on them.
- For most people, sex and gender match: they have the sexual organs of one sex, they consider themselves to be a member of that sex, and others around them think of and treat them as a member of that particular sex.
- People whose sex and gender do not match (they have the sexual organs of one sex but they think of themselves as belonging to the opposite sex) are referred to as **transsexuals**.
  1. Such a person would feel like a woman trapped in a man's body or like a man trapped in a woman's body.
  2. Transsexuals are not the same as **homosexuals** (individuals whose romantic and sexual interests are directed toward

members of their own gender), or **transvestites** (individuals who become sexually aroused by wearing the clothing of the opposite gender).

- In other cases, people may have the sexual organs of one particular sex and think of themselves as belonging to that sex, but when they interact with other people, they are **labelled** and **treated** as though they were members of the opposite sex.
  1. In such an instance, the gender of the person in question is difficult to categorize, because the personal and social components are not in agreement.
  2. Usually, this is not an issue; for the vast majority of people, how they identify themselves matches how others identify them.

Sex or gender differences: When sociologists study what is sometimes termed **sex** differences, **gender** differences are really the subject of examination.

- Sex belongs to the disciplines of **biology** or **anatomy**.
- Gender falls under the purview of **sociology** and **psychology**.

Key 49 Gender role identity and expectations

OVERVIEW *Most cultures have different norms regarding male and female behaviors. Culture, via the socialization process, teaches individuals the behaviors that are and that are not acceptable precisely because their gender is male or female in that particular culture. As people grow up, they are constantly faced with males-do-this (and they-don't-do-this) and females-do-that (and-they-don't-do-that) kinds of messages. This helps them form a lasting sense of what is considered proper and improper behavior for males and females in their culture.*

Gender role identity: This term refers to a personal belief that one should or should not act in a certain manner, based simply on whether the person is male or female.
- Gender role identity is a **personal** belief and attitude system that shapes and guides an individual's tastes and actions.

Gender role expectations: What society tells us we should or should not do simply because we are male or female in our culture.
- Much like gender role identity, gender role expectations represent the **social** or **cultural** belief and attitude systems that shape and guide all cultural members' preferences and behaviors, whereas gender role identity operates at the **individual** level.

Example:
- Frank believes that it is unmanly to cry and that real men should refrain from freely expressing sadness.
- Frank also believes that, in our society, it is a man's responsibility alone to earn the money to support his family.
- Frank considers it acceptable—maybe even expected—for men to watch sports on television all weekend, while their wives clean house, do laundry, and take care of the children's needs.
- As a consequence of these beliefs, when it comes to his own actions, Frank does not cry, rarely expresses negative emotions, takes care of his family, refuses to permit his wife to help support the family, and expects her to be solely responsible for the household chores.

- Taken together, these behaviors and preferences constitute part of Frank's gender role **identity**, because they represent the things that he, as a member of this culture, does and does not do based upon their appropriateness or inappropriateness for men and women in our society, as *he* perceives them.
- If society were to share Frank's beliefs and adhere to similar expectations for men's and women's behavior, then the gender role **expectations** for him as a male in this culture would be the same as his gender role **identity**.

Overlapping categories:
- There is usually an overlapping of masculine and feminine traits in a given individual: The key issue is whether masculine or feminine traits predominate for a given person in a given social context, and which traits are supposed to predominate for the person acting in a particular social context. *These* considerations determine how people will be treated as a result of their gender-related behaviors.

Key 50 Gender-appropriate vs. gender-inappropriate behaviors

OVERVIEW *Gender-appropriate behaviors are those things that are considered **acceptable** for males or females to do precisely because they are males or females acting in a particular cultural context. These are the types of activities in which we engage that are consistent with our culture's gender role expectations. Conversely, gender-inappropriate behaviors are those actions that are labeled as **unacceptable** because one is a male or female in his or her culture. They are the types of behaviors that run counter to our culture's gender role expectations; they are considered wrong or improper for men or women to do because they are men or women in our culture.*

Importance of gender-appropriate behavior: Sociological research on gender has consistently shown that the norms governing gender role expectations are among the strongest that regulate our lives.
- Most people prefer engaging in gender-appropriate behaviors even when doing so might be costly to them and inappropriate to a specific situation in which they find themselves.
- Most people are reluctant or unwilling to engage in gender-inappropriate behaviors even when doing so might be situationally acceptable or situationally proper.

Example of gender-appropriate behavior: Suppose that a woman finds herself attracted to a particular man and asks him out on a date.
- As a man of the 90s, he is flattered by her invitation and accepts the offer.
- The couple goes out for a nice dinner, enjoys the meal, and the check arrives.
- As a matter of habit, the man reaches for the check, but because the woman is the one who asked him out, she says, "No, I'm paying for this. I was the one who asked you out."
- The man feels intimidated by what he considers to be the

implications of having his meal paid for by a woman, and responds, "No, I'll pay for dinner."

- The couple goes back and forth on this a few times, with each person assuming responsibility to pay the bill.
- The problem: the man has chosen to engage in a gender-appropriate behavior (men pay for meals when they are on dates) that is inappropriate in this particular situation (it is expected that the person who asks for the date will pay, unless other arrangements were made in advance).

Example of gender-inappropriate behavior: Consider the situation faced by a 35-year-old man who is very close to both of his parents.

- Unexpectedly, his mother dies, and he is heartbroken over the loss of his mother.
- Throughout the entire process of making funeral arrangements, notifying family members about his mother's death, attending the viewing and the funeral, the man remains composed, never shedding a tear, even though he very much feels like crying.
- It is likely that people would consider it acceptable for him to express his grief by crying; and it is unlikely that they would think less of him as a man because he cried at his mother's funeral.
- By not crying, the man is refusing to engage in a gender-inappropriate behavior, even though the situation is one in which it might be acceptable for him to do so.

Key 51 Gender identity formation and core gender identity

OVERVIEW *Gender identity formation is the process by which we develop our senses-of-self as masculine or feminine beings. Core gender identity is the permanent definition of oneself as a masculine (male) being, or feminine (female) being.*

Gender identity formation: The process by which we begin to develop some ideas about who we are and about what we should and should not do because we are members of the male or female gender is referred to as gender identity formation.

- Our culture considers conformity to gender role expectations so important that the process of teaching us about the dos and don'ts of gender-related behaviors begins almost immediately in life.
- For most people, the process begins from the moment of birth, thus enabling us to get by in our society from a very young age.
- Once we learn the basics of how to conform to gender role expectations, little additional gender-related knowledge is needed.
- What additional knowledge is needed is only how to conform more easily in the variety of social circumstances in which we will find ourselves throughout our lifetimes.
- Once it has been formed, our gender identity remains largely unchanged, despite the fact that the process of refining gender identity continues throughout one's entire lifetime.

Core gender identity: Once developed, core gender identity remains with us for the rest of our lives; it is a lasting label that we apply to ourselves, to indicate that "I am a male" or that "I am a female."

- For almost all people, core gender identity is determined by ages 3 to 5.

- By the time we are three years old, most of us know that we are boys or girls, and we also have many definite notions of what males and females—including ourselves—should and should not do.
- These definitions of self, along with these notions of proper male and female behavior, remain with us for the rest of our lives, even though they were formed before we ever entered kindergarten.

Key 52 Gender influences during infancy

OVERVIEW *Because our society places such an extraordinary emphasis upon **acting appropriately** for our gender, our gender identity is continually being reinforced throughout our lives. This process begins at birth, during the infancy period.*

Gender differentiation: How males are differentiated from females is something that is **culturally** constructed.

- These differentiations are almost entirely **arbitrary**, and they can—and do—vary greatly from one culture to another.

KEY EXAMPLES

Most American hospitals still wrap their newborn males in blue blankets and their newborn females in pink blankets. Also, as soon as they are born, a bracelet reading "Male [surname]" or "Female [surname]" may be placed around babies' wrists, thus distinguishing which infants are which.

The act of naming babies is also gender-laden, since there are few gender-neutral names (such as Jamie, Kim, Kelly) in our culture.

- Even many of the names that are gender-neutral are often spelled differently for males and females (Tony if the person is male, Toni if the person is female; Terry if the person is male, Terri if the person is female).
- During the early childhood years, these naming differences will be utilized by the children themselves to place people into categories. By classifying all Kens, Mikes, and Davids in one category and all Julias, Annes, and Carolyns into another, children learn to associate themselves with a male or female kind of person.

Baby boys' rooms are often decorated in bright colors, while baby girls' rooms are more likely to be in pastels.

The "pink is for girls and sissies" notion that many adult American males have is attributable to these early-life gender influences.

Male infants receive more physical contact than female infants do, while adults speak to baby girls more than they speak to baby boys.

Baby girls are responded to more quickly when they cry than are baby boys.

It has been suggested that these and other similar differences lead to the later-life tendencies for men to be independent and inclined toward the physical, and for women to be emotionally expressive and inclined toward the verbal.

Key 53 Gender influences during childhood

OVERVIEW *The childhood period constitutes an important part of our gender development, because this period helps us to refine our **gender identities** beyond the initial notions of male and female behaviors that are set in our core gender identities. Many factors shape our still-evolving gender identities during childhood, among them: observing adults' behaviors, toys, books and school readers, television, and playtime encouragement.*

Observing adults' behaviors: Young people are likely to mimic the actions of others whom they see as their role models.
- Children are most likely to imitate the actions of their most-immediate authority figures—parents, grandparents, aunts, uncles, and teachers.
- Because these authority figures grew up in and continue to live in a culture that makes sharp differentiations between **proper** and **improper** behavior for males and females, they will usually demonstrate a number of gender-stereotyped behaviors.
- Consequently, when children observe and mimic these adults' actions, they begin to adopt many of their adult role models' gender-stereotyped actions for themselves.

Toys: Even today, many adults have stereotyped notions of what makes a proper boy's toy and a proper girl's toy.
- Boys' toys tend to be action-oriented (G.I. Joe action figures, Hot Wheels, Matchbox cars), extending and reinforcing the gender-related emphasis in the infancy period when boys were initially socialized to be more active and independent than girls.
- Girls' childhood toys, in contrast, are much more likely to be domestically related (baby carriages, Barbie dolls, Kenner Easy-Bake Ovens), along with a variety of home-related products.
- Even the coloring of these products' packages tends to be gender-stereotyped: Barbie dolls come in pink boxes; most dolls are sold in pastel colors that are usually associated with young ladies; boys' toy packages are usually very darkly or brightly colored.

Children's books and school readers: Content analyses of child-level reading materials reveal differences in how males and females are portrayed.

- Male characters significantly outnumber female characters in these books, sometimes by as much a ratio of 11:1.
- Male characters occupy a variety of roles and engage in numerous and diverse activities, whereas female storybook characters are almost always shown to be mothers, homemakers, teachers, nurses, or secretaries.
- The messages given to children are that:
  1. males are more important than females;
  2. males can—and usually do—have interesting lives filled with diversity; and
  3. females are more limited in what they can or should do (be a mother or homemaker, for instance).

Television: Once again, the message that males are different from—and in many ways, better than—females is transmitted **loud** and **clear** to children in the television audience.

- Like children's books, television programming also contains an abundance of male characters. Shows aimed at children are among the most uneven in terms of their male–female character ratio when compared to other types of television programs.
- Also like children's books, television shows present male characters in a wider variety of different situations, occupying a greater number of different roles, with proportionately more of these being higher-status roles than those depicted for female characters.
- With the average American child watching more than three hours of television per day, these gender-stereotyped messages are being received by children many times a day, every day, in an ongoing capacity throughout childhood. This strongly reinforces the socialization-related capabilities of the television medium.

Playtime encouragement: Many gender-related differentiations are made by parents and other role models regarding what children should and should not do during their leisure-time activities.

- It is more acceptable for boys to get dirty than it is for girls.
- Parents are more tolerant of their sons receiving minor injuries during play (scraped elbows or knees, bruises from falling) than they are of their daughters experiencing the same things.
- Boys are more likely than girls to be encouraged to roughhouse and to play physically.
- Certain games are considered more or less appropriate for boy or

girl children, for example, playing house is more acceptable for girls than for boys.

Cumulative effect: None of these occurrences alone is enough to instill gender norms in children; taken together, the cumulative effect is significant.

- Children are provided with consistent messages that **differentiate** boys from girls, and these messages reinforce the initial gender differentiation process that began during the infancy period.

Key 54 Gender influences during adolescence

OVERVIEW *Continuing the gender socialization process that was underway during infancy and childhood, several new factors crop up to reinforce gender roles during adolescence:* **peer** *norms,* **sexual prowess** *norms, asking for* **dates,** *and involvement in* **athletics,** *among others.*

Male-female differentiations: All of the following male-female differentiations have one thing in common: They all **reinforce** young people's perceptions that boys and girls are different, and that males and females have different **worths** in our culture.

Peer norms: These are extremely strong during adolescence.
- Probably at no time in our lives are we more conscious of what people think of us than we are during our teenage years.
- Probably at no time in our lives are we more sensitive to and concerned with what others think and say about us than we are during adolescence.
- During this period in our lives we are likely to be most rigid in our attempts to conform to gender role expectations.
- Gender role expectations seem to be particularly clear-cut and well-defined for adolescent boys.
  1. Labeling less-than-perfectly-masculine (less than overtly macho) males as "queers" or "sissies" or "faggots" is one of the ways that adolescents enforce gender norms.
  2. To be given one of these labels can be one of the most frightening and most highly stigmatizing things that can happen to a teenage male in our culture.
  3. Thus, there is a tendency for teenage boys to act in a **hypermasculine** way. This is an effort to prove to their peers that they are **real** males, acting appropriately for their gender.
  4. In so doing, teenagers are reinforcing their notions of what gender roles ought to be.

Sexual prowess norms: Along a similar line, sexual prowess norms clearly delineate gender norms for both males and females in adolescence.
- A very visible but very potent double standard is set up: In order

to conform to gender role expectations, teenage boys must appear to always be ready for sex.

1. They must always want sex, and must always emit an air of always being on the lookout for sexual opportunities.
2. Sexual prowess norms in adolescence demand that boys claim to be sexually experienced, or at least more experienced than their peers.
3. The norms for proper male behavior encourage boys to be walking, talking, breathing sex machines.

- The expectations for adolescent girls are very different.
  1. Unlike the boys, the girls are expected to reject boys' sexual advances, to make sure that they do not earn themselves a reputation for being loose or easy.
  2. Teenage girls are expected (much more than boys) to play hard to get.
  3. Above all else, girls are supposed to remain chaste.
- An intriguing paradox is thereby constructed: How are the teenage boys supposed to get all of their sexual experience when the girls are supposed to be virgins and homosexual contact is not considered an acceptable alternative? Our society is ill-equipped to grapple effectively with this dilemma.

Asking for dates: Another arena in which gender divisions are reinforced occurs in the adolescent period.

- Although things have changed considerably during the past 20 years, research shows that people still consider it more appropriate for a teenage boy to ask out a girl than for a teenage girl to ask a boy out.
- Studies of adolescent dating behavior suggest that boys are more likely to refuse a girl's invitation for a date than girls are to refuse a boy's invitation. Presumably, this occurs because boys feel that their masculinity has been threatened when a girl asks them out.
- Even in the 1990s, the gender-appropriate behavior is for males to do the asking and females to do the accepting or refusing when it comes to dating.
- Thus, dating behaviors serve as another way for gender roles to become more clearly defined.

Involvement in athletics: Like dating behaviors, this, too, is an area that has been undergoing change in recent years. There is greater equality among teenage males and teenage females now than in years past. Nevertheless, many key differences still exist.

- Boys' sports are better funded than girls' sports in most American junior high and high schools.

- Recent research on the sociology of sports indicates that attendance tends to be greater at male athletic events than at female athletic events.
- There is still a tendency for schools to offer a greater variety of sports to their male athletes than to their female athletes, thus leaving many teenage girls without the possibility of participation in the sport of their choice.
- Even today, many schools still separate boys and girls into different gym classes (as opposed to offering co-ed gym classes), sometimes even offering different sporting activities to the boys and the girls.

Key 55 Gender inequality in American society

OVERVIEW *As a sociological construct, the term **gender inequality** is used to refer to a systematic difference between the life experiences, social expectations, and opportunities that are available in life specifically because an individual is a male or a female. Our society makes **major distinctions** between men and women; and as a consequence, men and women face very different conditions as they go through their lives. These differences are numerous and can be quantified with several different measures.*

Different life experiences:
- Men, on the average, have it easier than women; there are numerous specific ways in which men have advantages when compared to women.
- The systematic, patterned nature of these differences has caused our society to be fraught with significant gender inequality.

KEY EXAMPLE

Education: Although the 1990 data show that women comprise a larger proportion of higher education enrollments than men do (54.4% vs. 45.6%), it is the women who are more likely to do so on a part-time basis (48.2% vs. 41.2%).

- The latter discrepancy is partly due to economic differences between men and women, which make it easier for men to be able to afford attending college on a full-time basis.
- This difference is probably also due, at least in part, to gender role norms in our culture that dictate that women be students **second** and mothers, wives, and homemakers **first**.

KEY EXAMPLE

Employment: Even today, women are more likely than men to be excluded from the labor force.

- Recent statistics suggest that women are nearly twice as likely as men to be nonparticipants in the labor force.
- This gap represents a significant improvement over the course of the past 30 years: In 1960, women were nearly four times as likely as men to be nonparticipants.
- By 1970, the four-times figure had dropped to slightly less than three-times.
- Since 1960, women have almost always had higher unemployment rates than men.
- At times, the male-female gap in unemployment rates has been small; in the past few years, for example, women's unemployment rates have been less than 5% higher than men's.
- At other times, the gap has been quite large; in 1970, for instance, women's unemployment rates were more than one-third higher than men's.

KEY EXAMPLE

Income: When they are employed, American women earn considerably less money than American men do.

- Today, the average working woman earns about two-thirds as much as the average working man.
- This is an improvement since the 1970s, when the average working woman earned a mere 60 cents to a man's dollar.
- Moreover, women are more than twice as likely as men to earn poor incomes (less than $4,000 per year). Men are more than twice as likely as women to be middle-income earners ($25,000–$34,999), and more than five times as likely as women to earn a good income (more than $35,000 per year).

Occupation: Even today, there are profound occupational differences between men and women in our society.

- Women are **under**represented in most of the jobs classified by the federal government as Managerial and Professional Specialty. These are the jobs that offer career opportunities, possibilities for advancement, job security, prestige, good salaries, and good benefits packages.
- Women account for less than 1/6 of all architects, 1/13 of all engineers, 1/3 of all math and computer scientists, 1/4 of all natural scientists, 1/5 of all physicians and dentists, and 1/5 of all lawyers and judges.
- At the same time, women are significantly **over**represented in the types of jobs classified as Technical, Sales, and Administrative Support or Service Occupations. In these jobs, men account for less than 1/5 of all health technologists (dental hygienists, radiology technicians), 1/40 of all secretaries, 1/8 of all information clerks, 1/12 of all bookkeepers, 1/26 of all child care workers, and 1/36 of all cleaning and servant workers.
- Ordinarily, the positions in which women predominate offer little job security, few if any possibilities for career advancement, very little occupational prestige, mediocre-to-poor salaries, and mediocre-to-poor benefits packages.

Theme 7 AGE, AGING, AND SOCIETY

This theme addresses some of the contemporary issues surrounding age and aging in American society. Like gender (discussed in Theme 6), age is a highly influential variable in determining how people treat others and are treated by others. This theme focuses on the demographic changes that are being seen in our society's age structure and why they are important from a sociological standpoint. This theme also examines some of the major life-stage models that have prevailed, and addresses what infancy, childhood, adolescence, and adulthood mean when these terms are used by a sociologist.

Key 56 Stability vs. change in the age structure of America

OVERVIEW *Is America stable or dynamic when it comes to the breakdown of various age groups in society? Do the proportions of all Americans who are teenagers or elderly remain fairly stable, or do these proportions change over time? The answer is quite clear: Across decades, the age structure of American society changes dramatically. Far from being stable in terms of its age composition, our society is **highly changeable.***

From 1980 to 2010:
- During this period of merely 30 years, the proportion of all Americans aged 17 or under is expected to experience a relative **decline** of 21.6 percent.
- The proportion of Americans aged 18–34 is expected to **decrease** by 22.4 percent.
- The proportion of Americans aged 45–64 will **increase** by 41.1 percent, while the proportion of those aged 65+ will **rise** by 23.0 percent.
- These are extremely large changes, especially when one considers that the time period over which these changes are occurring spans only slightly more than one generation.

Baby Boom generation: The 41.1 percent increase in the 45- to 64-year-old population is accounted for by what sociologists call the **Baby Boom** generation.
- This term refers to people who were born in the years following World War II (1945 to 1962).
- During these years, American birth rates skyrocketed as servicemen returned to America, rejoined their families or began the process of forming their families, and began having children.
- The birth years for the Baby Boom generation spanned an economically prosperous period in America's history, making it financially feasible for Americans to have large families.
- These years also corresponded to a conservative, traditional social atmosphere in our culture, which was conducive to having many children to perpetuate the values that are associated with family life.

- Consequently, Americans tended to have several children, and thereby created the largest generation in American history.

Baby Bust generation: In the years after the Baby Boom generation, there was a sharp **reduction** in American birth rates, dropping from a peak of 27 births per 1,000 women in 1947 to 14.5 births per 1,000 women in 1975.
- Over the course of less than two generations, the American birth rate nearly dropped in half.
- The sharpest part of this decline began in the middle 1960s, and continued throughout the middle 1970s.
- The result was an unprecedentedly small generation that some sociologists have called the **Baby Bust** generation, a generation that includes most students enrolled in college today.
- The shift away from having large families toward having fewer children is often attributed to such factors as:
  1. the rising divorce rate, which began to increase rather sharply during the 1960s;
  2. more economically demanding times than the 1950s, which made it unwise to have too many children;
  3. the Vietnam War, which meant that many young men of prime marriage and child rearing years were away from their wives and, hence, unable to begin their families; and
  4. a decline in the American cultural emphasis on traditional family values.

Baby Echo: In recent years, American birth rates have been on the **increase** again, although not nearly to the same extent as was seen during the Baby Boom years.
- This contemporary rise in the number of children being born has been referred to by some sociologists as the **Baby Echo**, which is usually attributed to the effects of the Baby Boom generation as they have begun creating their own families.
- What is perhaps most interesting about the Baby Echo generation is that it is larger than the one that preceded it, but only because the parenting generation is so large.
- Although the Baby Boomers are having fewer children per couple (on the average) than previous generations, there are so many Baby Boom parents in society who are having a child or two that the result has been a modest-sized upsurge in the newest generation in American society.

Key 57   The impact of the baby boom generation on American society

OVERVIEW   *The large Baby Boom generation has and will continue to have profound effects on our society in many areas, including the **labor force**, **consumerism**, and the **health-care** system.*

1970s: Some of the earliest of these effects were seen during the 1970s, as many of the Baby Boomers came of age and entered the work force for the first time.

- As a result of so many people entering the job market, jobs became difficult to obtain.
- During the early years of the Baby Boomers' coming of age (the 1960s), society was able to expand its job market sufficiently to accommodate most of the people who wished to work.
- After a decade of making such accommodations, our labor force was stretched to its limits.
- As a result, when the next push of Baby Boomers prepared to enter the labor force in the 1970s, there were few jobs for them.
- Consequently, unemployment rose sharply and remained high during most of the 1970s.

1980s: During the 1980s, the Baby Boom generation continued to affect American society, but in a new way: in the form of **yuppies** (originally an acronym derived from Young Urban Professionals).

- By the 1980s, the Baby Boomers were in their 20s, 30s, and 40s.
- These age groups cover American's greatest product-consuming years, and the years of the greatest use of entertainment and recreational resources.
- As a consequence, all sorts of new markets opened up, catering to the tastes and spending habits of this huge yuppie generation.
- Wine coolers, BMWs, designer water beverages (Perrier, Evian), the proliferation of cable television programming, upscale outdoor restaurant-cafes, and numerous commodities became the benchmarks of yuppie success.
- All of these commodities thrived because they appealed to the

large Baby Boom generation, which took liberal advantage of their availability and demanded more and more such amenities.

Future: In the years to come, the Baby Boom generation will continue to have a **sizable impact** on our society.

- This effect will probably become most profound between the years 2015 and 2050, when the Baby Boomers start entering old age and retirement. ,
- Current population trends suggest that the elderly population will at least double within the next several decades, due in great part to:
  1. advancing medical technology and
  2. the aging of the Baby Boom generation.
- Our social welfare and health care systems for the aged are already facing economic hardships, and the prognoses for these programs are poor.
- As medical technology continues to enable people to live longer, and as the Baby Boom population bubble moves into the ranks of the elderly, these services will become increasingly important.
  1. Who will pay for the Medicare and Medicaid needs of the elderly when there are so many more of them?
  2. How will we provide adequate hospital care for the more-than-doubled number of people aged 65 or older in the years to come, when we can barely provide adequate hospital care for them now?
  3. Who will pay for these people's medical insurance and hospitalizations?
  4. How will the already overburdened nursing home and long-term care-facility systems adapt to a doubling of the elderly population?
- These questions represent crucial dilemmas that our culture must resolve in the years to come. They are all the result, at least in part, of a society that has an **unstable age distribution** of its population.

Key 58   The impact of the baby bust generation on American society

OVERVIEW   *If having an unprecedentedly large genera-tion makes things difficult in society because the social structure is poorly equipped to accommodate such a large generation of people's needs, other types of difficulties arise when a generation is unusually small. As was true for the Baby Boom generation in the 1970s, the effects of the Baby Bust generation began to appear in the 1980s. Probably the Baby Bust generation's two greatest areas of impact to date have been on the **educational system** and in the **work force**.*

Educational system: With the small numbers of people occupying the Baby Bust generation, it has often been difficult to fill classrooms in many parts of the United States.

- Class sizes, at an all-time high in the 1960s and 1970s, began to diminish in the 1980s as the Baby Busters progressed through the ranks of school.
- Suddenly, some schools (those that had been expanded or constructed to accommodate the Baby Boom generation) were unable to justify their existence in view of diminishing enroll-ments. As a result, some school districts had to consolidate in order to remain financially solvent.
- In many areas, teachers had to be laid off from work because their positions, which were essentially expansion positions that had been created one generation prior to compensate for the Baby Boom children, were no longer necessary.
- In recent years, as the older Baby Bust children have entered college, these effects have carried over into the postsecondary educational experience.
- In many colleges, enrollments are down, despite the increasing emphasis in American society on obtaining a good education, because there are fewer college-aged people than there were 10 or 20 years ago.
- Consequently, competition for the better-qualified student appli-cants has increased sharply in recent years; many colleges and

universities have been struggling to make ends meet with fewer students.

- No doubt this trend will continue for several more years, as the most-recently-born of the Baby Busters enter college, and as the enrollment difficulties shift from the undergraduate education level to the graduate education level.

Work force: The Baby Bust generation's influence has been—and continues to be—considerable in this arena as well.

- As a result of the Baby Boomers' exit from entry-level positions, many jobs have been left vacant and unfillable because there are fewer people in the Baby Bust generation to assume their positions.
- Minimum wage jobs appear to have been among the hardest-hit; the availability of such jobs has been widespread for several years.
- As a result, many employers who, during the Baby Boom generation years, offered prospective employees few benefits and poor salaries are finding themselves forced to offer more attractive salaries and benefits packages to potential employees.
- The small size of the Baby Bust generation has contributed to these problems.

Retirement: When the large Baby Boom generation reaches retirement age and finds itself in need of social and health-related services for the aged, the small Baby Bust generation will be of prime working age.

- The Baby Bust generation will be contributing the tax dollars for providing services to the Baby Boomers, and soon, America will experience a time when a small generation is forced to support a large generation.
- This cannot be done effectively with the tax and public assistance structures operating the way they currently do. We will need to devise a strategy for caring for the elderly in the decades to come, not only because there will be so many more older Americans, but also because the pool of potential supporters of the elderly will be so small.
- This problem is another of the side effects of America's dynamic age population.

social conceptualizations of
life stage

OVERVIEW *From the time we are born until we die, we spend our lives passing in and out of various life stages. During each stage in our development, society has different expectations for us regarding what we should and what we should not do. During different life phases, we have different* **responsibilities***, we are offered different* **opportunities***, and we must make different types of* **decisions** *in our daily lives. Consequently, if we wish to understand the social norms that govern our lives at various points throughout our lives, it is important to develop an understanding of the socially defined or recognized stages through which people pass during the course of their lifetimes.*

Five life stages: Sociologically speaking, our culture recognizes only five life stages:

> infancy
> childhood
> adolescence
> adulthood
> old age

Previous life stage perceptions: This developmental schema has not been in existence for very many years. In fact, two of these five stages, **adolescence** and **old age**, were not recognized in any meaningful way until the 20th century.

- During the mid-1800s, people matured from **infancy** to **childhood** to **adulthood**.
- There was no period of **adolescence** as we now know it. Because people typically died young, there was no life stage representing **old age** as we currently know it.
- There is considerable evidence, based on archival content studies of letters, marriage documents, personal diaries, and nonfiction

stories, to indicate that about 100 to 150 years earlier, there was no **childhood** stage as we now recognize and label it.

- During that era, people progressed directly from an infancy period into an adulthood phase, where they remained until they died.

Reconceptualizing the life stages: As society changes, so do society's definitions of what life stages there are.

- As new norms develop to govern our everyday lives, life stage models must keep pace by reconceptualizing the birth-to-death process.
- The next several keys explain how this process has taken place over the course of the past few centuries.

Key 60 Before there was a stage of childhood

OVERVIEW *During the 1600s, there were only two distinct life stages in existence in our culture: **infancy** and **adulthood**. The stages that we now call **childhood**, **adolescence**, and **old age** were unknown at that time.*

Definitions of infancy and adulthood:
- Infancy was the period in one's life when people were too young to be able to work and contribute to the family's subsistence.
- As soon as people were old enough to make a significant contribution to the family's household and/or employment-related needs, they entered **adulthood**.

KEY EXAMPLES

- If a young person of age five were physically capable of helping with the family's chores, and if the family came to rely upon this individual's contribution to the everyday routine of the household, then that five-year-old would, in most respects, be considered an adult in the life-stage model operating at that time.
- If, on the other hand, another 5-year-old were very small and fragile, hence incapable of making a significant contribution to the household's chores, then that person would remain an infant despite being the same age as the one who was deemed an adult.

Age disparities in adulthood: It was not age per se that determined individuals' life-stage classification; rather, it was the types of things that they were capable and incapable of doing that determined whether they were to be categorized into the infant or adult stage.
- In most ways, culturally defined adults were treated as peers, despite occasionally huge age disparities.

Influence of death rates:
- The stages of childhood and old age were most likely unrecognized during this period because high death rates in America

kept those segments of the population from growing into significant numbers.

- During the 1600s, the typical American did not live to see a fortieth birthday.

  1. At the time, most Americans died as the result of acute illnesses that were untreatable or incurable, not because their bodies deteriorated as a result of old age.

  2. The prolonged years of physical decline that we now associate with old age were relatively rare three centuries ago.

- Death rates among the very young were also high at this time in America's history.

  1. In colonial America, approximately 50 percent of newborns did not live to see their twelfth birthday. Consequently, many parents were reluctant to develop deep-seated emotional attachments to their young offspring.

  2. Many did not invest themselves in their children's psychological well-being or emotional development because this was often an unwise investment of their own personal emotional energy.

  3. It was only after young people passed the critical age of thriving that parents could feel certain that their offspring would be an ongoing part of their lives.

  4. Thus, the nurturance that we associate with childhood today was not typically provided for the young of 1600s America. Young people of that era were not seen as special beings who should be coddled and sheltered and protected, as children of today are.

Key 61   The addition of childhood to the life-stage process

OVERVIEW *For reasons that are not entirely clear to contemporary scholars, American adults' notions of the early years of life appear to have undergone some important changes from the late 1600s to the early 1800s. Three specific examples can be provided to support this idea. They pertain to the manner in which children were **dressed**, artistic renditions of **family life**, and the expansion of our **educational system** for the young.*

Dress: The first change that seems to have taken place toward the turn of the 18th century was that many parents, particularly those from the upper-middle and upper socioeconomic classes, began dressing their offspring differently, based on the age of the children.

- Prior to the change, all youngsters who belonged to the infant category were dressed similarly, regardless of whether they were newborns or four-year-olds.
- Around 1700, a differentiation came to be made in the dressing of less-than-seven-year-old offspring and older-than-seven-year-old offspring. How and why such a distinction in attire initially came about is subject to speculation.
- The implication of the differentiation, however, is clear: America was seeing the beginning of a new way of thinking about young people; they were not being lumped together into the infant category.
- By having two ways to dress their different-aged young, adults were indicating that they also viewed these youngsters (infants and children) differently.

Depictions of family life: The second change that took place around the turn of the 18th century was the way artists depicted family life, particularly in those settings in which young people were present.

- Prior to the change, artistic portrayals showed game-playing, merriment, and frivolity as belonging in the realm of **adulthood**. Rarely, if indeed ever, were young people shown playing games or enjoying themselves.
- With the change, young people were occasionally shown to be

playing games; increasingly often, they were shown having fun and doing frivolous things simply because they were enjoyable.

- The change in the ways that youths were depicted by artists reflects a change in the way adults of the time viewed young people.
- This change probably contributed to the formation of the stage that subsequently became known as **childhood**.

Expansion of the educational system: Finally, and perhaps most significantly, America witnessed a proliferation of its educational system toward the end of the 1700s and during the early part of the 1800s.

- Prior to this time, education was minimal for most Americans. For most, obtaining an education was unimportant; people could learn from their parents everything they needed to know about how to survive and earn a living.
- As social conceptualizations of young people changed, the young were divided into two categories—**infants** (as previously designated) and a new group that would eventually become identified as **children**—and society began to treat these types of youngsters differently.
- Increasingly, it became attractive to send the youngsters in some families to school, where they learned a few potentially useful life skills.
- This provided a clear point of differentiation for infants, children, and adults: Infants were **too young** to attend school; adults were **too old** to attend school; only children were to be sent away to receive an education.
- Initially, the schools to which young people were sent were catchalls for all of America's children. They were not **age-graded**; that is, they did not divide the youngsters into different groups based on age and on skills that people are presumed to have mastered by a certain age.

If a five-year-old and a twelve-year-old were sent to a particular school, they sat side by side and were responsible for learning the same materials as one another.

- While this seems ludicrous to us today, it is important to realize that at the time, the five-year-old and the twelve-year-old student were not perceived differently from one another:
  1. Both were beyond the infancy period.
  2. Neither was participating on a full-time basis in adult-like responsibilities or activities.
  3. Both were attending the same school and studying the same curriculum.
- As a result, both were categorizable as belonging to the **childhood** phase.

Key 62 The addition of adolescence to the life-stage process

OVERVIEW *With time, the American educational system became increasingly organized, complex, and gradiated. Initially, the one-room, one-curriculum-for-students-of-all-ages school of the 1700s gave way to a two-classes-present-in-one-room schooling system. A distinction was made between* **less-experienced learners** *and* **more-experienced learners.** *By dividing America's schoolrooms in half, our society was, essentially, dividing the childhood period in half. It was as though childhood consisted of two subphases that could be differentiated on the basis of the amount of knowledge that young people had gained. This set the stage for the addition of a new stage to the developmental model: the stage of* **adolescence.**

1700s: Initially the division into two classes in a particular school was traceable not to the ages of the students, but rather to the students' previous **exposure** to education.
- Newer students were separated from those who were more experienced, so the latter could be provided with an advanced curriculum.

1800s: The educational reformers of the 1800s suggested that America's educational system would become more effective if it provided guidelines about **when** people should enter school.
- This led to changes in the schooling system, eventually resulting in the highly age-graded educational system that prevails in our school system today, where second graders learn things to expand upon the knowledge that they gained in first grade, and where third graders are expected to advance upon their second grade learning, and so on.

1900s: It was not until the beginning of the 20th century that adolescence even remotely began to resemble the life stage that it now is.
- The first of several 20th-century factors leading to the development of adolescence was the **Great Depression.**

1. During this time of prolonged economic hardship, America expected its **children** to attend school, in the hope that they would obtain knowledge and skills that would eventually enable them to compete more effectively for jobs in American society.

2. Society typically had different expectations for its **adolescents**, who were expected to drop out of school and get a job to help support their families.

3. During this time, **infants** were those individuals who were too young and immature emotionally and physically to attend school, and **adults** were those individuals who were old enough, skilled enough, and mature enough to be self-supporting.

- A similar differentiation between children and adolescents was made during **World War II**.

1. With their fathers away at war, many older offspring left school to enter the work force due to economic exigencies. As in the Depression years, this was necessary so that the families could make ends meet.

2. In the process, **children** came to be viewed as those young people who were not yet able to contribute to the family's subsistence, while **adolescents** were those who were capable of making such a contribution.

3. While adolescents were expected to help support their families, they were not afforded full **adult** privileges. They continued to be subservient to their parents, and were not treated as adults, even though they were engaging in adult-like behaviors.

4. America was telling these young people that they were old enough to make a difference, but not yet old enough to be considered full adult citizens. They were no longer children, yet they were not yet adults—they were **adolescents**.

- It was not until the 1950s that adolescence began to resemble the life stage as we know it today.

1. Contemporary life-stage scholars often attribute the modern conceptualization of adolescence to two things: **television** and **rock-and-roll music**. The proliferation and growing popularity of these media in the 1950s provided teenagers with a culture all their own.

2. Certain television programs were designed to appeal specifically to a teenage audience.

3. Rock-and roll-music gained genuine acceptance and popularity, primarily among teenagers.

4. Younger children were typically disinterested in this music and in its associated dance crazes; adults tended to be repulsed by the sound of what many of them called *the noise* of drums and guitars.

5. For the first time in American history, youths were provided with something that they could call their own—something that clearly appealed to them and something that distinguished them once and for all from their younger siblings and from their parents.

6. A culture of adolescence was established, and it firmly entrenched adolescence as a life stage within contemporary life-stage models.

Key 63 The addition of old age to the life-stage process

OVERVIEW *Unlike the additions of childhood and adolescence to the life-stage model, **old age** became a full-fledged life stage unto itself very gradually. Throughout America's history, there have always been a certain number of elderly people in society, although the definition of what constitutes elderly would vary at different times in our history. But when being old and infirm is an exceptional phenomenon rather than a fairly common occurrence, old age cannot be said to constitute a life stage. Such was the case until sometime in the 20th century. Only when the numbers of people reaching elderly status increased substantially and when physical deterioration due to advancing years became widespread, were we able to say that old age evolved into a life stage all its own.*

Changes in life expectancy: In all likelihood, old age as a new life stage first occurred sometime within the past 50 to 75 years.
- At the turn of this century, the average American's life expectancy was only 47 years.
- In 1900, it was a genuine rarity when someone lived beyond the age of 70; to do so was to live 50 percent longer than average.
- Today, the average American's life expectancy is more than 75 years.

Roles of medicine and gerontology: The addition of old age to the infant→child→adolescent→adult model can be attributed to advances in the fields of **medicine** and **gerontology**, which is the scientific, holistic study of aging and of the elderly.
- Advances in medicine are directly responsible for the substantial increase in life expectancy that has been seen in our culture during the past century.
- Advances in gerontology brought about more interest in the field in the 1970s.
  1. Developing understandings of the psychological, social, and medical needs of the elderly; the psychology of old age; and the social psychology of the aging process are among the major

goals of gerontological research. These goals have become increasingly important as the aged population has expanded in size during the past 20 years.

2. A focus of academic attention on old age (that is, the existence of gerontology as a major specialization area) was an indicator that something new was occurring; enough people were affected by the phenomenon in question that it merited specialized attention by researchers.

3. The expanded interest and research in aging-related issues will probably continue well into the next century.

4. With an increasing number of gerontologists finding acceptance for their work, old age has become more widely accepted by others as a life stage unto itself, distinct from adulthood, middle age, and the so-called preretirement years.

Key 64 Youth as a new life stage?

OVERVIEW *For the past 40 years, our culture has been using an infant→child→adolescent→adult→old age life-stage model, despite the numerous social changes that have taken place in our society. In considering the dynamic nature of our contemporary culture, some scholars have contended that this model is no longer adequate to account for the life-stage process for certain people.*

Difficulty in classifying certain people: Life-stage models operate under the assumption that all people can be classified, on the basis of their **age** and, more directly, on their **responsibilities** and **activities**. There are certain people, however, who are difficult to place in one of the existing categories.

KEY EXAMPLE

Think about how a 20-year-old college student majoring in biology with a B grade average would be classified.

- Labeling this person an adolescent implies relative immaturity: an individual who is faced with few responsibilities and is frequently irresponsible, and who lacks a direction in life. These are the traits that our culture associates with adolescence.
- For the serious, academically-inclined, career-oriented student mentioned above, the label **adolescent** does not apply.
- Neither is the label **adult** likely to fit this person either. In our culture, **adult** implies someone who is financially self-supporting, employed full-time, married (or in a serious relationship), and emotionally mature.
- For the most part, these traits do not apply to most college students today.
- If we must categorize the biology student, knowing that this person is not an unusual or exceptional example in today's society, then we must reconsider the validity of the current life-stage model in use.

Youth: One of this writer's contributions to the life-stage literature is the suggestion that scholars consider the possibility of there now being a new life stage, termed **youth**, falling between the currently recognized stages of adolescence and adulthood.

- The youth stage applies only to those people who engage in some **organized, extended activity** after leaving high school and before entering the labor force on a full-time basis.
- A youth period would be experienced by those individuals—now in the majority in this nation—who choose to attend **college** and to those who enlist in the **military** for a few years, among others.
- Creative persons (artists and writers, for example) who **travel** extensively in order to build an experience base on which they can draw professionally might also be classified as youths during their travel/ experiential period.
- The traits that distinguish youth from adolescence and young adulthood all have one thing in common: They all relate to providing delimited responsibilities.
- During the college, or military service, or travel years, people begin to experience real responsibility and independence, often for the first time in their lives, but they experience these things in a tentative way. Society does not confer upon them the full rights to responsibility and independence that will be granted to them in adulthood.
- Youths, then, are allowed to make **some** of their own decisions and to begin taking control of their lives (unlike adolescents), while simultaneously having their parameters for potential error limited (unlike adulthood).

Examples: This message of delimited responsibility is conveyed to people during youth in the following ways:

- The presence of resident advisors and hall counselors in college student dormitories to provide support for people that may need help.
- Living expenses (rent, food, utilities) are normally not the financial responsibility of young people in these circumstances.
- Jobs.
  1. Adolescents are often **permitted** to work, but it is expected and acceptable that their jobs will be dead-end jobs that offer little more than work experience and spending money.
  2. Adults are **expected** to work and their jobs are expected to offer advancement, job security, a decent income, and, at best, personal fulfillment.
  3. Youths are **occasionally permitted** and **occasionally required** to work, and their jobs resemble a combination of these traits:

mediocre pay, good work experience, occasional career opportunities.

- Future planning.
  1. Adolescents are not expected to plan for their future, other than in a vague and tentative way.
  2. Adults are expected to look toward their future at all times, making all of their decisions with the potential implications in mind.
  3. Youths are expected to consider the future when making decisions, but doing so recklessly or making a mistake in future-related plans are both tolerated by society.

Key 65 Sociological vs. psychological conceptualizations of life stage

OVERVIEW *One major difference distinguishes the sociological models of life stage from the psychological models: the level of* **complexity** *characterizing them. In almost all instances, psychological models of development are more intricate than sociological models, the former involving a great many more developmental stages than the latter.*

The sociological model: Our society currently recognizes a five-stage sociological developmental model: **infancy, childhood, adolescence, adulthood, old age**.

The psychological models: These vary depending upon the theorist; but because they are based on a combination of the theorist's notion of **intellectual**, **perceptual**, and **emotional** development, very fine differentiations are made.

- Developmental psychologists speak of life-stage differences among infants; toddlers; early-, middle-, and late-stage children; preadolescents; early-, middle-, and late-stage adolescents; young, mature, middle-aged adults; preretirement-period adults; and young-, middle-, and old-old groups of aged people.
- This psychological model contains 15 or 16 distinct life stages, each of which is claimed to be differentiable from all others.

Explanation for differences:
- Sociological models of life stage are based on how people are **treated by others** in society, what others **expect** of them, and what their **responsibilities** are at different times in the course of their lives.
- **Example**: As a culture, we tend to treat children of all childhood ages more or less alike, regardless of whether the child is aged five or ten.
- As a culture, we tend to have similar expectations for children and do not differentiate too much among their responsibilities,

regardless of their age within childhood. Sociologically speaking, a child is a child is a child.

- Psychologically speaking, the five-year-old and ten-year-old are at different points in their cognitive, emotional, and perceptual development; developmental psychologists would, in all likelihood, categorize these children into different life stages.
- Psychologically speaking, then, a child is *not* a child is *not* a child; rather, one must examine each individual's **cognitive**, **emotional**, and **perceptual** developmental levels in order to classify the child into the most appropriate life-stage category.
- The same rules could be stated for adolescents, adults, and elderly persons.

Theme 8 SOCIOLOGICAL ASPECTS OF RACE AND ETHNICITY

*T*his theme provides the reader with an overview of issues pertaining to race, ethnicity, and racism in contemporary society. The initial keys address the distinction between race as a biological concept and as a sociological concept, and examine meaningful racial classifications. The next several keys in this theme address the racial composition in American society and changes that are being seen in the racial make-up of the United States, what racism is, and how racism and racial inequality are manifested in our society. From there, the attention shifts to discussions of ethnicity and the difference between race and ethnicity. The theme concludes by presenting several models to explain the American cultural response to ethnic group diversity.

INDIVIDUAL KEYS IN THIS THEME	
66	The biological meaning of race
67	The sociological meaning of race
68	Meaningful racial groupings: Do they even exist?
69	Racial composition and major race-related population trends in America today
70	Racism

Key 66 The biological meaning of race

OVERVIEW *Biologically speaking, race is determined on the basis of a group's **blood line**. Race is a constellation of physical differences that have resulted from the adaptations that human groups have had to make to the environmental conditions in which they have lived. The existence of different racial groups is the result of long-term processes in which climactic conditions initially caused specific physical traits to develop in a certain people. Once these traits developed, they became part of that people's gene pool because the individuals tended to marry one another and have children with one another.*

Effect of climactic conditions on physical adaptation of two races:

- The dark skin that we see in people that we refer to as members of the **black** or **African-American** race is a **physical adaptation** that these people's ancestors' bodies made to the climactic conditions in which they lived.
- Tens of thousands (or more) of years ago, these people's ancestors lived in the tropical and subtropical parts of Africa, where the sun is very strong year-round.
- As a result of being exposed to the potent, dangerous rays of the sun for prolonged periods of time on a daily basis, these people's bodies were forced to undergo a change in order to keep them protected (for example, from skin cancer).
- Consequently, through an evolutionary process, their bodies came to produce larger amounts of melanin, a substance that darkens the skin and protects it from some of the sun's damage.
- Since this physiological change was an **adaptive** one for people living in this part of the world, it became part of the **gene pool**.
- As these individuals married other people living in this region, all of whom were very slowly developing darker and darker skin tone, and had children with them, the darker skin color was passed down through the ages. In the process, the black or African-American race was formed.
- In other parts of the world in (the **Scandinavian** region, for example) the sun is much weaker.

- Natives of this part of the world did not need the same amount of protection against the sun's rays as those people living in the more equatorial regions did, and their skin tone evolved in such a way as to appear very light.
- Because certain essential vitamins are provided by exposure to the sun, developing a lighter-than-average skin tone might have been an adaptive mechanism, when these people's skin became fairer, it made them more susceptible to the sun's rays.
- By virtue of living in a very different climate and facing very different environmental conditions than their more equatorial resident counterparts, the **Caucasian** or **white** race was formed in the northern regions of the world.

Key 67   The sociological meaning
of race

OVERVIEW   *When sociologists talk about **race**, they are referring to a large number of people who, for social or geographical reasons, have tended to intermarry and interbreed with one another over a long period of time. As a result of these marriage and childbearing patterns, these persons have developed **specific physical characteristics** that are passed down from generation to generation in the gene pool. In these ways, the biological and sociological notions of race are much the same. Sociologists, however, take the concept further, because a race is also something that involves a **labeling** process and an **identification** process. Sociologically speaking, it is not enough that these people share certain physical traits. They must also identify themselves as being individual members of a much larger group whose members are somehow alike, perhaps even united, by virtue of their physical similarities. The sociological notion of race also involves a labeling process by others in society, whereby these outsiders categorize individuals into specific groups based on their physical characteristics.*

Sociological definition of race:
- To a sociologist, race is more than a series of biological characteristics; it entails a way of thinking and identifying oneself.
- Race also incorporates the way that people are **categorized** and **treated** by other people in their culture.
- These categorizations and ways of treating people are typically based on personality and behavioral traits that are thought to be associated with belonging, or not belonging, to a specific racial group.
- As a sociological concept, race is a **social fact** because people judge others and make assumptions about others based on their beliefs and attitudes about what people of this or that color are like.

KEY EXAMPLE

Consider a young woman whose mother is white and whose father is black. As a result of the mixed-race blood in her, this young woman has a darker skin tone than we would typically associate with Caucasians, but a lighter skin tone than we typically associate with blacks.

- Biologically speaking, this woman is 50 percent white and 50 percent black in terms of her racial classification.
- Sociologically speaking, though, if we wish to classify this woman into a racial group, we must understand how her physical characteristics affect her day-to-day life.
  1. To what race do people think she belongs? Based on the answer to this question, how is this woman treated by others?
  2. How does she identify herself? When she thinks of herself, does she think of herself as black, as white, as biracial, or in some other way?
  3. What implications does this have for her and for how she feels she ought to live her life in our racially divided culture?
  4. All of these questions are relevant to understanding race as it pertains to this woman's situation, and make race a more complicated concept to sociologists than to biologists.

KEY EXAMPLE

Vanessa Williams is another example of the complexity inherent in the sociological meaning of race. In the late 1980s, Ms. Williams, who identifies herself as a black American, was chosen Miss America. Because she is very fair-skinned, many people were unaware of her racial identity at the time of her crowning.

- Shortly after being crowned, Ms. Williams mentioned that she felt particularly proud to act as a role model for black female youths.
- Members of the media and most of the American public had not thought of (**labeled**) Ms. Williams as a black person. They had mistakenly assumed that she was Caucasian, and treated her as

though she were the latest in a long succession of white Miss Americas.

- When her self-identification as a black Miss America came to people's attention, though, the focus of many interviews with her shifted.
- Once people became aware of her racial identity, they treated her somewhat differently.
- Here, race became an issue where it had not previously been considered. Society made it an issue for this particular Miss America.

Key 68 Meaningful racial groupings: Do they even exist?

OVERVIEW *From a **biological** standpoint, the answer to this question is probably best answered with a qualified yes: i.e., there are certain types of physical traits that are found in large numbers of people because these people have, for extensive periods of time, married and had children only with other people sharing their physical traits. The world over, the tendency has long been for people to marry and procreate within recognized racial boundaries. **Sociologically** speaking, there is no question that meaningful racial groups exist. Our society seems to be especially prone to dividing people into various categories based on their **shared physical attributes**, and then treating them differently.*

Concept of racial purity:
- The number of individuals who are 100 percent racially pure (those for whom **no one** in their **entire** ancestry has ever had a child with a member of another race) is likely to be very small.
- Across the hundreds of generations that comprise a person's total biological lineage, the chances are extremely slim that there will not have been **at least** one ancestor of another race.
- Technically, then, biological classifications of race do exist, but they are misleading to some extent. If, for instance, someone is one-eighth black and seven-eighths white, is it completely correct to label this person's race as white?

Five major racial groups:
- In America today, we typically recognize the following major racial groupings:
  1. **white** (Caucasian)
  2. **black** (African-American)
  3. **Hispanic** (Latino or Chicano)
  4. **Native American** Indian (also includes Native Alaskans)
  5. **Asian** (also includes Pacific Islanders).

- One of these sociological racial classifications, Hispanic, is actually an **ethnic** classification, not a racial categorization per se.
- Hispanic is considered one of the major racial groupings because our culture tends to put people of Hispanic descent into one category, to make certain assumptions about them based on their purported group-level similarities, and to treat them accordingly.
- Thus, even though Hispanic is technically an ethnic group classification, it is also a meaningful racial grouping for such people in our society *because our culture makes it a meaningful racial grouping.*

Key 69 Racial composition and major race-related population trends in America today

OVERVIEW *Regarding its racial composition, America is overwhelmingly white (**Caucasian**). Today, people who are white comprise 84.4 percent of the U.S. population. An additional 12.3 percent of all Americans are **black**, 8.1 percent are classified as **Hispanic**, and 3.3 percent as **Native American** Indians. (NOTE: Hispanics can also be counted as black or white, with these figures thus totaling more than 100 percent.)*

Population trends for various racial groups:
- Far from remaining stable, the racial composition of our society has been undergoing significant changes, and the current trends are predicted to continue for **at least** the next two decades.
- Higher birth rates among blacks and Hispanics are leading to increases in those proportions of the American population.
- Concomitantly, the proportion of the total population that is white is decreasing.
- As recently as 1980, white people comprised 85.9 percent of the U.S. population (1.5 percent higher than today), while blacks constituted 11.8 percent of the American populace (0.5 percent lower than today) and Hispanics 6.4 percent of the U.S. population (1.7 percent lower than today).
- Demographers predict that by the year 2010, the U.S. population will be 81.1 percent white (representing a relative decline of 5.6 percent over the 30 year period in question), 13.7 percent black (representing a relative increase of 16.1 percent between 1980 and 2010), and 10.9 percent Hispanic (representing a relative increase of 70.3 percent over the 30 year period in question).
- As is true for the age composition of American society, our nation's population structure is also dynamic when it comes to its racial make-up.

Key 70 Racism

OVERVIEW *The phenomenon of racism is so complex, involving so many different components and being manifested in so many different ways, that developing one all-encompassing definition of racism is difficult. There are many ways of defining racism, each of which captures certain aspects of the phenomenon while ignoring others. In discussions of racism, it is useful to understand the various definitions of the term.*

Definition based on domination and exploitation: One way of defining racism incorporates the concepts of **domination** and **exploitation**.

- When such a definition is used, racism is viewed as the domination or exploitation of one large group of people by another large group of people, simply because the latter group feels that the former group is **inferior** in some way on the basis of its race.
- This way of thinking about racism builds on the notion that racism involves a struggle between relatively **powerful** and relatively **powerless** groups in society, whereby the former represent the racial majority.
- The basic idea is that racism occurs whenever the majority group chooses to exercise its **power** over the minority group, simply because it is able to do so.
- This definition of racism also implies that racism does not exist unless the majority group takes advantage (that is, dominates or exploits) the racial minority group.
- One of the weaknesses of relying upon this particular definition of racism is that it fails to provide sufficient consideration of the **attitudinal** components that most of us associate with racism.
- The definition's primary strength lies in its implication that racism entails the disadvantaging of one group by another simply because of the former's physical (racial) traits.

Definition based on ideology and attitude: An alternative definition of racism might focus more on the **ideological** and **attitudinal** aspects of the phenomenon.

- When most of us think about racism and about what makes someone a racist, we are usually drawn to the idea that the racist's **beliefs** and **attitudes** about people of another skin color differ from those of the nonracist.

- What makes someone a racist may or may not be the things that the person does; rather, a racist is someone whose beliefs and attitudes toward people of another race are **negative** and **disparaging**.
- Accordingly, an alternative definition of racism might conceptualize racism as an unfounded, unwarranted, or unreasonable **hatred** of one group by another, based on perceived differences in the abilities and worths of the group's members.
- There is an implication that one group feels that it is superior to another, and that the other group's purported inferiority is in some way attributable to its racial make-up.
- This definition of racism focuses on the notion that racists think that they are more capable than people of a different skin color or that they are **more valuable** to society than these other people are.
- This definition of racism not only emphasizes the existence of **negative** feelings toward a certain group because of its racial characteristics, but also the **strength** of these feelings.
- Implicit in such a conceptualization of racism is the notion that, having these beliefs and attitudes about another group, the people adhering to the racist sentiments will be more likely than those who do not have such beliefs and attitudes to act upon their convictions, with the implication that racists will probably engage in certain types of behaviors against certain people, specifically because of their race.

More comprehensive definition: Perhaps the best way to think of racism is to employ a definition that synthesizes the key elements of **both** of these conceptualizations of racism.

- In our society and in practically all other societies where racism exists, racism involves **beliefs, attitudes**, and **behaviors**.
- Racism can be said to exist whenever someone **judges another person negatively** or whenever someone **does something negative** to another individual specifically because that person belongs to, or is thought to belong to, another race.
- Racism can occur in the presence or in the absence of overt **discriminatory actions** against a second party; and conversely, discrimination can take place in the presence or in the absence of overt racist **attitudes** regarding a particular person or group.

Key 71 Three conditions that must be present for racism to exist

OVERVIEW *Racism appears whenever some people, presumably identifiable on the basis of their shared physical traits, believe that they have or that they ought to have more than some other group, which, presumably, is also identifiable on the basis of shared physical traits. It occurs when people feel that there is an inequity in the social system and that some members of society have advantages, necessities, or amenities that others do not have (but should have); thus, the fuel for racism is provided.*

Three conditions must be met for racism to exist:
- Two groups must coexist, and they must be **identifiable to** and **distinguishable from** one another on the basis of their visible physical characteristics.
  1. If the groups do not coexist, the jealousies and dissatisfactions that fuel racism will not be found.
  2. If the members of these racial groups are not sufficiently identifiable to and distinguishable from one another, people would not know which people to like and which to dislike on the basis of their racial characteristics.
- These groups must be in some sort of **competition** with one another.
  1. This competition can be for any number of things, including land, goods, power, and prestige, among others.
  2. When certain people feel that they are entitled to more than others, or when some groups feel that they and others like them have been disadvantaged in some systematic way, the racism fires are stoked.
  3. Thus, when some people feel the need to compete with others in order to get what they want, need, or feel entitled to, racism may result.
- Finally, the groups must be **unequal** in **power**.
  1. If members of both groups hold **equal power** in society, then both groups can dissolve and minimize their opponent's racist

beliefs, attitudes, and actions before they lead to actual overt manifestations of racism.

2. With equal power, the stigma that accompanies being a racial minority group member can be averted, because one is able to **retaliate** or mobilize one's own forces to counterbalance the racist tendencies of one's accusers.

3. With equal power, one group's beliefs and attitudes cannot prevail over another's.

4. Thus, it is the **inequality** between the competitive groups that provides the final element necessary for racism to develop and thrive, especially if racism is to take on the behavioral rather than merely the attitudinal manifestations.

Key 72 Concrete manifestations of racism and racial inequality in American society

OVERVIEW *A distinction exists between **racism** and **racial inequality**. Racism involves adhering to beliefs and attitudes that are negative or disparaging to some group of people specifically because of their race or perceived race. It may also entail engaging in actions that are damaging to and/or discriminatory against some group because of its members' physical characteristics. In contrast, **racial inequality** is a systematic difference in the life experiences, social expectations, and opportunities that people have available to them in life specifically because they belong to, or are thought to belong to, a particular racial group.*

Racial inequality as a consequence of racism:
- When people have certain **negative** beliefs and attitudes toward a particular racial group, and when they engage in certain types of behaviors as a result of these beliefs and attitudes, clear-cut differentiations are made between members of different races.
- When this happens on a widescale basis and when these differentiations tend to be of relatively long duration (that is, when they become systematic and patterned in society), then racial inequality will exist.
- Some sociologists consider racial inequality to be yet another type of racism, referred to as **institutional racism**, which is defined as the systematic denial of opportunities and rewards because of an individual's classification by others in positions of power and authority.

Concrete manifestations of racial inequality: Members of different racial groups face very different life chances and are given, or prevented from availing themselves of, very different opportunities.
- **In education:**
  1. In America today, the average black person has 12.4 years of education, the average Hispanic person 12.0 years and the average white person 12.7 years.

2. While the intergroup differences are not large, on the average, American whites are better educated than their black and Hispanic counterparts.

3. Today, blacks have high school dropout rates that are more than 25% higher than those seen among whites; Hispanic dropout rates are more than two-and-a-half times higher than those of whites.

4. Education is one of the few measures of racial inequality that has shown an improvement over the past 20 years.

- **In employment:**

1. Hispanic individuals currently have an unemployment rate nearly 75% higher than that seen among whites, while black unemployment rates are two-and-a-half times those of whites.

2. Even today, blacks and Hispanics are significantly underrepresented in the types of occupations that offer good incomes, good benefits packages, job security, and possibilities for advancement, while simultaneously being overrepresented in occupations that pay more poorly, offer few benefits, offer little job security, and have few possibilities for advancement.

3. Blacks and Hispanics comprise less than half their proportionate share of the managerial and professional specialty positions in the United States (engineers, doctors, lawyers, scientists), but they account for considerably more than their proportionate share of such jobs as cleaning and servant work, mail and message distribution, and health service work.

4. These differences have worsened since 1980, a change that is typically attributed to the funding cutbacks that Ronald Reagan implemented during his term in office as U.S. president.

- **In standard of living:**

1. Standard of living measures indicate that blacks and Hispanics have a lower standard of living in American society today than whites do.

2. Currently, the average black person earns 57 cents to the white person's dollar. The average Hispanic person earns 71 cents to the white person's dollar. Both of these ratios are down, not up, from the comparable figures in the 1970s.

3. Similarly, black people are more than twice as likely and Hispanic people more than one-and-a-half times as likely as white people to earn an annual income below $9,999.

4. In contrast, blacks are about one-third as likely and Hispanics about half as likely as whites to earn an income greater than $50,000 per year.

5. Black and Hispanic people alike are at least three times more likely than Caucasians to be living in poverty today.

6. This situation has worsened, not improved, since the 1970s.

- **In criminal justice:**

1. Examining some data for race and crime, inequalities are again plentiful.

2. Black people are arrested at a rate that is more than two times greater than that among whites. This gap has widened since the middle 1970s.

3. Black and Hispanic individuals are overrepresented in the prison population, by more than one-half for Hispanics and by about a factor of three for blacks; this difference has not changed much since the late 1970s.

4. Blacks are much likelier than whites to be victimized by crimes. The most recent data available suggest that blacks are nearly 50% more likely than whites to be victims of a violent crime, suffering from a robbery rate that is about 2.5 times higher than that seen among whites, a rape rate that is about 4 times higher than among whites, and a murder rate that is more than 6 times higher than among whites. Blacks also have more than a 50% greater chance than whites do of being victims of burglary.

Trends toward increased racial inequality: When all of these measures are put together, the picture that is drawn is a bleak one where racial equality and racial tolerance are concerned.

- Our society is extremely unequal in terms of race, and many of these differences are getting worse rather than better.

- Consider the consequences of these trends, especially if they continue in the years to come, as blacks and Hispanics will comprise a larger and larger proportion of the American populace.

- One of the unspoken implications of these measures of racial inequality is that our society is moving in a direction of creating sharp social chasms between the haves and the have-nots.

- When this is seen, increased racism is fostered, which in turn often leads to increased racial inequality.

Key 73 Racial groups and ethnic groups

OVERVIEW *Racial groups and ethnic groups are **alike** in many ways. Both involve large numbers of people. Members of both groups tend to marry and to have children with members of their own group. Members of both groups are often identifiable to others on the basis of physical characteristics and social behavior. Both groups come to think of themselves as belonging to a much larger group of people who, by virtue of their shared racial or ethnic characteristics, are like them. Racial groups and ethnic groups simultaneously **differ** from one another in the following way: Racial groups are determined by the physical traits passed down genetically from one generation to another; ethnic groups are identified by their cultural traits.*

Similarities:
- Part of what makes a racial group or an ethnic group is not merely how the individual members **label** themselves, but also how others in society label them on the basis of what is thought to be their race or ethnicity.
- Both involve large numbers of people who tend to marry their own kind and to have children with their own kind.
- As a result, both racial and ethnic groups pass down certain **physical characteristics** from one generation to another, often making members of these groups somewhat identifiable to others.
- Members of a racial group or ethnic group identify themselves as belonging to a much larger group of people who are like them.

Differences:
- **Race** is rooted in **biological** characteristics; ethnicity is rooted in characteristics associated with **culture** and **heritage**.
- **Ethnicity**, by definition, involves a sharing of culture and certain cultural traits, rather than merely sharing physical traits (skin color, eye shape) that can be passed down genetically from one generation to another.

- In everyday parlance, ethnicity is often referred to as **nationality**, meaning the specific country or region of the world from which one's ancestors came, for example, Italian, Irish, Pakistani, Japanese, Australian, Scandinavian, European, or Hispanic.
- When sociologists distinguish between ethnicity and race, they are usually interested in focusing on the kinds of beliefs, attitudes, and values that people have, and the types of behaviors in which they engage specifically because they were raised with these as part of their cultural heritage.
- Far beyond simply passing down one's physical characteristics through the generations, ethnic groups also transmit knowledge of "the Old World," and instill into the newest generation's members the importance of adhering to these "Old World ways."
- Many stereotypical behaviors that we tend to associate with certain cultural groups are actually manifestations of these groups' ethnic heritage.

KEY EXAMPLES

Cultural traits: The stereotypical Italian mother's emphasis on eating (epitomized by the phrase, "Mangia, mangia!") is said to be indicative of such a person's ethnicity.

Such traits as "Jewish guilt," bowing by Japanese women when they enter and exit a room in which a male authority figure is present, and daily usage of wine in France, make up one's ethnicity.

- The personal association with these types of traits or (more importantly) with the cultural group that inculcates these traits into its members, makes an ethnic group what it is and serves to differentiate it from a racial group.

Key 74 The Anglo-conformity approach to dealing with ethnic group diversity

OVERVIEW *Of the various ways that Americans have responded to ethnic group diversity, the Anglo-conformity approach is clearly the least tolerant. Under this approach, people coming to America with the hope of becoming a naturalized (American) citizen must abandon all of their Old World ways and replace them with traits that are acceptable in American society.*

Description of the Anglo-conformity approach: Under this approach, the immigrants are expected to abandon most of their Old World **institutions**, their Old World **customs**, and their Old World **traditions**—their entire ethnic cultural identity—in favor of those that are more obviously American.

- New arrivals are generally expected to relinquish their native tongue and begin speaking English.
- Our society usually grants people a short length of time in which they are permitted to alternate between their native language and English, as long as they are making what is considered a good-faith effort to become fluent in English.
- As time goes on, such individuals' use of languages other than English—especially in public places—will be tolerated less and less, and is likely to be met with a number of unpleasant reminders (dirty looks, rude comments about "speaking the language") that one is, indeed, breaking the American cultural norm of speaking English.
- Under an Anglo-conformity model, ethnic group diversity is considered a type of **deviancy** and is treated accordingly.
- Like most types of deviants, ethnic group members who do not conform to the American norms and to the American ways of life are shunned, labeled negatively, and sometimes even stigmatized.
- When an Anglo-conformity approach is used, little (if any) effort is made to merge the various cultures or to enable groups with

different backgrounds or different values to coexist peacefully with one another.

- The assumption is made that these groups will live together in harmony when—but only when—the newcomers act like the native residents. It is also presumed that this is an acceptable way of treating people who are not originally from America.
- The prevailing attitude under an Anglo-conformity model can be captured by the phrase, "If you don't like the way we do it here, then you can just go back where you came from!"
- Of the various ways that we, as a culture, have used to respond to ethnic group diversity, this approach is the one that has been most commonly used *and* the one that has had the longest staying power in our culture over the course of the past century and a half.

Key 75   The melting-pot approach to dealing with ethnic group diversity

OVERVIEW   *Unlike the intolerance that is represented by the Anglo-conformity approach to dealing with ethnic group diversity, the **melting pot ideology** is decidedly more tolerant. This model assumes that there will always be significant ethnic group diversity in our culture, and that diversity enhances American culture and improves the overall quality of life in America.*

Description of the melting-pot approach: Far from discouraging immigrant groups or individuals with a strong ethnic heritage from retaining their ethnic identities, the melting pot ideology encourages people to keep in touch with their cultural roots, while simultaneously recognizing that this will be difficult for them.

- The melting-pot approach assumes that much of a given individual's ethnic heritage will be lost in the **assimilation** and **acculturation** processes.
- Unlike the Anglo-conformity approach, the melting-pot approach takes the view that there is no such thing as an ideal person—no traits and behaviors that make some people more desirable than others.
- Under the melting-pot model, the ideal person is one who is an amalgamation of many **different ethnicities**, and whose beliefs, attitudes, values, and behaviors reflect the very finest qualities of **several ethnic heritages**.
- The term *melting pot* originated with the idea that our society is like a big pot of stew.
  1. Every day, many new ingredients are added to the stew, changing the overall flavor that the stew has.
  2. The ingredients are groups immigrating to America, each bringing its own **belief** and **attitudinal structures**, its own **value system**, and its own unique **cultural heritage**.
  3. These latter four characteristics represent the factors that change the flavor of the stew, and America's geographic boundaries represent the pot in which the stew is made.

4. Just as a stew has a flavor all its own, a flavor that does not really resemble any of the individual ingredients making up the stew, but rather the unique blending of flavors that results from their combination, so too will our society develop a flavor (or a characteristic) all its own, based on the summative effect of these various ethnic groups' contributions to our culture.

- Through increased **cultural diversity**, America will become better, because the true American would be a transglobal human whose beliefs, attitudes, values, and behaviors reflect the best of what the world's cultures have to offer.

Key 76 The cultural pluralism approach of dealing with ethnic group diversity

OVERVIEW *The **cultural pluralism approach** to dealing with ethnic group diversity represents an **ideology** that is neither as intolerant and absolute as the Anglo-conformity model nor as idealistic and optimistic as the melting-pot notion. The cultural pluralism approach allows people of different ethnicities to retain their ethnic heritages and all of the beliefs, attitudes, values, and behaviors that come to them from their ethnic background.*

Description of cultural pluralism approach: Under such an approach, different ethnic groups do not have to give up their Old World ways or beliefs or their attitudinal or value systems; nor are they expected to convert to the dominant cultural position in their new homeland.

- Under a cultural pluralism model, **ethnic group variations** are supported by the society-at-large.
- The guiding ethos is one of **respect** for others' ways of life, and **tolerance** of others' beliefs, attitudes, and values, even if they differ from one's own.
- Unlike other approaches, the cultural pluralism model insists on a system that operates on the principle of **separate-but-equal** regarding various ethnic groups.
- The cultural pluralism model involves a **laissez-faire** (or hands-off) approach to dealing with ethnic group diversity.
- Each group is supposed to continue on with its own ethnic traditions, living life as its members see fit; it is expected that the greater society will respect this.
- Society-at-large does not make an effort to **assimilate** these various groups; it does not try to change people or their ways of life; and it does not try to enable people to live together more harmoniously in spite of their differences.
- Different ethnic groups never truly become integrated into the greater society, because by retaining its ethnic customs, each group retains a sense of **separateness** and **differentness** from all others.

- Under such a model, various ethnic groups tend not to feel connected to one another or to the society-at-large in which they are living.
- Cultures that operate with a cultural pluralism model tend to experience periodic problems between different ethnic groups, because these groups' **values** frequently conflict with one another.
- Groups are often unable to relate to one another, because the separate-but-equal nature of pluralistic cultures prevents the various groups from developing genuine understandings of one another's beliefs, attitudes, values, and behaviors.
- Often these differences are so large that these groups divide into ethnic neighborhoods that isolate and insulate their members from others in society who do not share their ethnic heritage; examples are New York City's Little Italy and various cities' Chinatowns.

Theme 9 SOCIAL STRATIFICATION

*T*he purpose of this theme is to examine the concept of social stratification and to see how people's lives are affected by this complicated social phenomenon. The theme begins by explaining the concept itself, and then discusses the relationship between social stratification, social class, and life chances. From there, several major stratifiers are discussed, with emphasis placed on how these factors affect one's social position. The theme concludes by examining two very different types of social systems, closed and open, and explaining how they are based on systems of stratification.

Key 77 Social stratification

OVERVIEW *Social stratification is **patterned social inequality**. Saying that the inequality is patterned indicates that the differences occur: 1) on a widescale basis, 2) with regularity, and 3) along the lines of certain specific, identifiable characteristics (e.g., race, gender).*

Social stratification defined:

- **Patterned** tells us that if we know whether a person or group possesses or does not possess certain traits, then we will be able to predict with reasonable accuracy how this person or group is likely to fare in the social hierarchy.
- **Social inequality** means that some types of people systematically experience advantages in society while other types of people are systematically disadvantaged in our society.
  1. Some members of our culture can be thought of as **haves**, and others can be thought of as **have-nots**.
  2. The determination of who is to be socially advantaged and who is to be included among the ranks of the socially disadvantaged is based, in part, on certain characteristics these individuals possess and, in part, on how society values or devalues these characteristics.
- Social stratification affects people's lives and can be manifested in various ways in society. (See Keys 78, 79, and 80.)

Key 78 Life chances and social class

OVERVIEW *People are divided into different groupings and their lives are structured accordingly. There are certain things that some people cannot do, simply because their station in life prevents them from being able to do them. Other people, in a different social stratum, are able to do these things specifically because they occupy a more favorable position in the social hierarchy.*

Social inequality and life chances:

- Social inequality is a **structured** and **systematic phenomenon** that affects people in the various social classes throughout their lives.
- By virtue of patterned inequality in society, social stratification affects people's **life chances**.
- Life chances are the **opportunities** that individuals do or do not have to engage in certain activities, and the opportunities that they do or do not have to accomplish certain goals simply because of where they are located in the social hierarchy.

KEY EXAMPLES

Some people are born into very wealthy families that are able to send them to the finest private schools to obtain the finest available education.

Other children of equal intellectual capacity are born into families that are poor, preventing them from being able to obtain such a fine education.

- The **intellectual capabilities** of the former children are maximized, whereas the latter children's abilities are probably not nurtured as well because of the lesser quality of the schools to which they are sent.
- The child from the wealthy family thus has a head start in life when compared to the poorer child, even though both children started out with **equal innate abilities** to succeed.
- The children began their lives with different life chances because

of the different positions in the **social structure** they and their families occupied.

- Different life chances are, therefore, the result of social stratification.

Social class: People who can be considered peers in society because of their similar life **chances**, similar life **circumstances**, and similar **opportunities** constitute a **social class**.

- Sociologists usually conceptualize American society as consisting either of three or nine distinct social classes.
- In the **three-class model**, our society is divided into a lower class, a middle class, and an upper class.
- In the **nine-class model**, each of these classes is further divided into three subclasses: a lower-lower class, a middle-lower class, an upper-lower class, a lower-middle class, and so forth.
- As a general rule, the three-class model makes more meaningful sociological distinctions among people based on their life chances than the nine-class model does.
- The nine-class model does a better job of recognizing the nuances among the specific social class positions that people in our society might occupy.

Example: The income gap between someone who is designated as lower-middle class and someone who is upper-middle class might be $50,000 per year.

- In the three-tier model, both individuals are categorized as middle-class members.
- While this may be true categorically speaking, it ignores the fact that the latter person, by virtue of the extra $50,000 available each year, is able to do many things and enjoy many amenities that the former person cannot.
- The nine-tier model is capable of recognizing this difference and highlighting its potential significance for the lives of the people involved.

Key 79 Ascribed traits as social stratifiers in American society

OVERVIEW *Social stratification is determined on the basis of a number of variables, each of which can cause someone to be advantaged or disadvantaged compared to others in society. It is not the impact of any one variable that leads to one's social class position in America; rather, it is the unique combination of stratification-related factors that one possesses that determines how one fares in our culture's social hierarchy. Some of the traits that characterize us are within our own control; over other traits, we have little, if any, control. The former types of traits are referred to as **achieved traits**; the latter are known as **ascribed traits**.*

Major ascribed social stratifiers: Sex, **race**, and **age** are three major ascribed social stratifiers, but there are many others.

Sex: We cannot control whether we are born male or female, yet whether one is born male or female will have a profound effect on that individual's life.
- Compared to men, women are disadvantaged in many ways in our society.
  1. Women earn less money, on average, than men do.
  2. Women almost always have higher unemployment rates than men do.
  3. Women are overrepresented in the types of jobs that pay poorly and that offer few possibilities for career advancement, while simultaneously being underrepresented in those jobs that pay well and offer prestige, job security, and career opportunities.

Race: People cannot choose what race they are, yet one's race is likely to have a profound effect on social standing.
- Social class lines tend to be sharply divided by race.
- Blacks and Hispanics have fewer years (on the average) of **education** than whites do.

- Blacks and Hispanics today are considerably more likely to drop out of school than whites are.
- They have higher **unemployment** rates than Caucasians do.
- On average, blacks earn much **less money** than white people do; as a consequence, they are significantly more likely than white people to live in poverty.

Age: We cannot control how old we are, yet age affects how we are treated by society.

- Typically, advantages go to people who are in the mature adulthood life stage, aged 30 to 44.
- When people are younger than age 30, our society often discredits them somewhat on the basis of their youthfulness and on the basis of their lack of life experience.
- This often means that adolescents and young adults must work doubly hard to attain anything more than minimal recognition for their skills and accomplishments.
- In some instances, they must work extra hard just to be given a chance to try or achieve certain things.
- At the same time, our culture also discriminates against people who are middle aged or older (approximately 45 and older).
- While we do not devalue middle-aged adults on the basis of inexperience or having insufficient life experience, our tendency is to label these people "past their prime" or "over the hill."
- The tendency toward discreditation is perhaps most apparent with respect to how we treat the elderly (those aged 65 and older). These individuals are given little credit for their knowledge, experience, and skills; in fact, it is frequently—and incorrectly—assumed that their memory and skills are on the decline even when there is no objective evidence to support such a contention.

Key 80 Achieved traits as social stratifiers in American society

OVERVIEW *Achieved stratifiers are those traits 1) that affect our position in the **social hierarchy** 2) over which we have some degree of **control**. Many such variables exist; three important ones are educational attainment, having a criminal record, and marital status.*

Educational attainment: Although opportunities for higher education are not equally available to all people in our society, education is something over which most of us do have *some* measure of control.

- For example, all of us can determine whether or not we attend classes, whether or not we ask questions when something is unclear, how close we pay attention in class, how dutifully we do our homework, how diligently we study for our exams—all factors that are related to educational success.
- With the expansion of higher education in American society in recent decades, most people who have applied themselves to the learning process prior to high school graduation have options for further education available to them later in life.
- Although the grades that we receive are not entirely within our control, certainly our efforts and performances are relevant to the grades awarded us.
- Research has shown that education is related to the type of job that people get, and that it is also related to the average amount of money that people earn. Educational attainment thus becomes a source of **social stratification**.

Criminal record: Having, or not having, a criminal record is another achieved stratifier in our culture.

- People who have been convicted of a crime, particularly if it was a felony, typically face life-long difficulties, prejudices, and discriminations in our society.
- Many Americans seem to operate with a "once a criminal, always a criminal" ethos that makes it difficult for people who have been found guilty of a crime to resume a normal life ever again, even if they have served their full sentence.

- The fact that someone has a criminal record is given so much weight in our culture that it attains what sociologists call a **master status**.
- A master status is an identifying label that carries with it such potent messages about and implications for the person who has been labeled that the label alone comes to dominate other people's perspectives of the individual.
- Once labeled as a **criminal**, the person is thought of as a criminal who has served a sentence, or as a criminal who is no longer imprisoned, or as a criminal who probably cannot be trusted, or as a criminal who now wants to get a job.

Marital status: When marital-status labels come to affect how people are treated by others, stratification is often a result.
- In certain social circles, it is considered unacceptable or less desirable for people to be **single**.
- When adopting children, it is considered preferable if one is **married**.
- When applying for a bank loan, especially a large one, it is better to be married than to be single.
- Married people are presumed to be more stable and more responsible than single individuals.
- Many automobile and life insurance policies operate with this assumption as well.
- In decades past, there was a strong social stigma in our culture against people who were **divorced**; such individuals were labeled and treated by others in society as failures.
- In many contemporary corporate settings, it is expected that up-and-coming executives will be married or, at the very least, in the sincere pursuit of a lifemate. Being single is sometimes considered bad for the company's image, signifying that there is something wrong with the unmarried person.

Key 81 Open social systems

OVERVIEW *All societies can be classified into one of two types, **open** social systems or **closed** social systems, based on how flexible or rigid they are when it comes to social stratification and social mobility. In the open social system, social class differentiations are usually easily identified, but the lines dividing classes are not clearly drawn. Although it is not always easily accomplished, movement from one class to another is possible.*

Description of open social systems:
- People usually have to struggle to keep their foothold in the social hierarchy. If they do not work hard, they risk losing their social class standing and may drop a class level or more.
- People have an incentive to work hard because they are told that if they apply themselves, work hard, and succeed, they may be able to improve upon their station in life.
- Open social systems are usually characterized by a great deal of **competitiveness**, because the haves and the have-nots coexist and see what it is like to be the other kind of person in our society.
- The have-nots are told that all they need to do to become one of the haves is to work hard; the haves are threatened with loss of their "have" status if they do not work harder than— or at least hard enough to maintain their distance from—the have-nots.
- If and when the gap between the haves and the have-nots becomes too great in an open social system, **social upheaval** occurs because people feel that they are not being given a fair chance at attaining success and equality in society.

Examples of societies that have open social systems:
- The United States of America. Although there is typically little movement from one social class to another in America, it is classified as an open system because the possibility, not to mention the promise, of advancement from one class to another is present and is not prohibited by any formal societal mechanisms preventing upward or downward social mobility.
- Most—if not all—of the European nations.
- Most—if not all—of the so-called Western nations.
- Numerous "Third World" nations.

Key 82 Closed social systems

OVERVIEW *In a **closed social system**, which is also referred to as a **caste system**, social class differentiations are easily identified and the lines between classes are sharply drawn. The social structure permits little or no movement from one class to another. In a closed social system, people are born into a particular social class, and except in unusual circumstances, can expect to remain there for the rest of their lives.*

Description of a closed social system:
- **Upward social mobility** is impossible.
- When closed systems are considered, the term for the different stratification groupings is **caste**.
- **Hard work** does not lead to improvement in one's social class (caste) standing; and being **gifted** or possessing special, extraordinary **talents** does not increase one's likelihood of moving up in the social hierarchy.
- **Downward mobility** is a possibility, albeit a remote one, when someone violates a more or law that mandates reduction in social standing as part of the punishment for the moral or legal infraction.
- In order to maintain such a rigid and unyielding social class system, closed social systems tend to be run by powerful, authoritative, repressive governments.
- Without **strong ruling bodies**, the class/caste boundaries would become less distinct, hence subjecting the entire system to potential change.
- Change and social mobility are so minimal in closed social systems that these types of societies tend to be relatively **stable** over time.
- In this way, closed social systems differ from open social systems, which tend to be dynamic and highly susceptible to social change.

Example: Perhaps the best modern-era example of a closed social system is India, which, for centuries, has been divided into a complex **caste** system.
- The uppermost caste is known as the **Brahmins**, who are

considered to be the most pure and the most elite within Indian culture.

1. They constitute India's nobility, its privileged or ruling class.
2. The Brahmins are expected to have nothing whatsoever to do with lowly tasks; this type of work is considered to be beneath them.
3. Except fraternizing with or consistently befriending the Untouchables, there is nothing that Brahmins could do to lose their privileged status in Indian society.

- At the bottom of India's caste structure is a group known as the **Untouchables**, who are considered impure, almost to the point of being deemed contaminated.

1. The Untouchables are only permitted such low-level occupations as waste removal, for they and they alone are considered worthy of such a task.
2. Traditionally, the Untouchables have been forbidden to have certain kinds of contact with the Brahmins, and risked losing their lives if they violated these societal expectations regarding their proper place in society.
3. There is nothing that an Untouchable could do to lose the status as society's dregs.

- The caste society permits no caste changes, particularly regarding upward social mobility.

Theme 10 DEVIANCE

*T*his theme focuses on the important concept of deviance, and examines it from a sociological point of view. The first two keys address the distinction between concrete and normative deviance. From there, a brief discussion explains what the sociology of deviance includes. The remainder of the theme concentrates on several principal theories of deviance. These keys are designed to familiarize the reader with various ways that sociologists examine deviance and the different ways that deviance can be understood from a sociological perspective.

Key 83 Concrete (statistical) deviance

OVERVIEW *There are two types of deviance. **Normative deviance** is anything that occurs contrary to the folkways, norms, mores, or laws in existence at the time. While this type of explanation of deviance is not necessarily incorrect, it is not necessarily correct either. **Concrete** or **statistical deviance** does not make reference to folkways, norms, mores, or laws. Some examples of concrete deviance do not entail the violation of social expectations, but on the contrary, they may entail desired or desirable things.*

Definition of concrete deviance: Any characteristic, behavior, or social phenomenon that occurs so rarely that, when it does occur, it can be considered unusual.
- With concrete deviance, there is an implied reference to a statistical mean (something is deviant when it is significantly different from the mean), or to the everyday, the ordinary, the commonplace (the norm).
- A deviant characteristic, behavior, or phenomenon is any characteristic, behavior, or social phenomenon that is significantly different from the **norm**, significantly different from the **mean,** significantly **out of the ordinary**, in terms of the frequency with which it occurs.

KEY EXAMPLE: Characteristics that qualify as concrete deviance:

- Because most people have blue or brown eyes, those rare individuals whose eye color is hazel have an eye color that may be described as deviant in the sense of concrete deviance.
- Because brown, black, and blonde hair are the norm, someone who is born with natural red hair has a hair color that exemplifies concrete deviance.
- Being ambidextrous rather than being left-handed or right-handed also qualifies as an example of concrete deviance.

None of these characteristics—all of which are examples of deviance—even remotely implies something that goes against social expectations of propriety or legality.

KEY EXAMPLE: Behaviors that can be described as concrete deviance:

- Imagine that you are driving along an interstate highway that has a speed limit of 55 miles per hour.
- You are driving 50 m.p.h.—a behavior that is perfectly legal—but as you cruise down the road, you are passed by car after car.
- Speeding is so much the norm nowadays on American highways that the person who actually drives at or slightly below the speed limit is engaging in a behavior that is deviant in the concrete sense.
- Notice that no law or more was broken, and there was nothing illegal in what you, as the driver, did.

KEY EXAMPLE: Social phenomena that can be described as concrete deviance:

- Imagine that it is early afternoon on a Tuesday in mid-July, and you decide to go shopping at the local mall—ordinarily, a quiet time of the day and a quiet day of the week for shopping.
- Much to your surprise, however, you notice that the mall is packed, much like it would be at Christmas time.
- After asking around about the hubbub, you discover that your favorite luxury store is having an "Everything Must Go" 90% discount sale—hence, the crowd at the mall.
- This situation provides two examples of concrete deviance, in finding that
  1. the mall is crowded during the early afternoon on a Tuesday in July (which is very unusual), and
  2. your favorite luxury store, which almost never reduces its prices, has significantly slashed its price tags.
- In these examples, something has been described as deviant without implying anything negative about it.

Key 84 Normative deviance

OVERVIEW *Anytime an individual's actions run counter to the societal expectations governing a particular social context, that person has engaged in a behavior that can be considered **normative deviance**. Sometimes normative deviance involves a serious infraction (such as breaking a felony law), whereas at other times it may involve a minor transgression (going against a folkway). Sometimes norms or mores may be governing a situation, dictating clearly what is and what is not considered acceptable. In yet other situations, the behavioral expectations may be codified in laws that specify precisely what is and what is not permissible.*

Four examples: Each involves the violation of a different level of societal expectation for conformity (**folkway**, **norm**, **more**, and **law**).

KEY EXAMPLE ONE

Suppose that one of your professors came to class one day wearing bright red pants.

- The pants were in conformity with the university's dress code, and constituted appropriate—albeit loud— attire, but they were so brightly colored that you and your classmates found it difficult to concentrate on the class lecture.
- The professor has done something that exemplifies normative deviance because he has violated a **folkway** (wearing apparel that is not distracting to one's students in class).
- Like concrete deviance, normative deviance does not always involve breaking a law or doing something that people consider wrong; it simply means that someone has done something in violation of societal expectations.

KEY EXAMPLE TWO

Imagine that you are sitting in class and the two people sitting directly behind you constantly whisper and giggle during the lectures. Every day, they distract you and other students, because their conversations and laughter make it difficult to hear.

- These students are engaging in a type of normative deviancy; they are violating the classroom **norms** of sitting quietly and attentively, and not being a disturbance to others.

KEY EXAMPLE THREE

Suppose that you have a next-door neighbor, a 30-year-old single mother with two children, aged 5 and 8. One day, she leaves her young children at home alone while she runs some errands.
- Before leaving for the store, she impresses upon her kids the importance of being on their best behavior and of not opening the door for any strangers while she is out.
- She makes sure they understand her, and she leaves, locking the doors on her way out. She is gone for about two-and-a-half hours.

- As a neighbor, consider how you would react to such a situation, especially in light of the ages of her children.
- Most people would be concerned (at a minimum) or outraged at the mother's actions, claiming that she was wrong to leave such young children unattended for such a long period of time.
- Typically, this woman's behavior would not be in violation of any laws; but she has done something that violates a **social more**—namely, that of providing adequate protection and care for her children.
- By leaving her children alone and thereby violating this particular more, this woman has engaged in a type of normative deviance.

KEY EXAMPLE FOUR

Consider the case of an arsonist who has been found guilty of burning down his father-in-law's home after a domestic dispute. This person is now imprisoned and sentenced to ten years in jail for his offense.

- Because all laws are reflections of societal expectations for behavior, whether they are minor (laws governing jay walking) or major (laws regarding murder or rape), all violations of **laws** can be considered examples of normative deviance.
- The arsonist, then, engaged in a type of normative deviance when he set his father-in-law's house ablaze.

Key 85 What does the sociological study of deviance include?

OVERVIEW *The term deviance has such a broad meaning that the sociological examination of deviance is necessarily diverse. Numerous deviance-related subdisciplines exist within the broader academic discipline of sociology. The following list of topics will give the reader some idea of the breadth of subject areas that constitute the sociology of deviance: deviance **theory**, **alcohol and drug** studies, **criminology**, **sexuality** research, **racism**, **sexism**, and **ageism**.*

Deviance theory: Theory is one of the most important areas in this academic sector. Entire books and edited collections of essays and articles have been published on the subject, focusing only on the authors' specific conceptualization schemata or theories of deviance.

Alcohol and other drug studies: The sociological research in this field examines such things as how alcoholism **affects** the lives of people who interact with the alcoholic, how society **responds** to people with alcoholism or other drug dependencies, what factors in the social structure **influence** drinking or other drug use patterns, and others.

- Whenever alcohol or other drug studies examine use-related problems or pathologies, or when they entail investigations of the relationship between certain types of unhealthy or dysfunctional attitudes and subsequent drug-use-related behaviors, they are focusing on the **normative** aspects of drug usage.

- Because **deviance** from norms and **conformity** to norms usually co-occur, the research in this field often exemplifies the sociology of deviance.

Criminology: The relevance of the sociology of deviance is more readily apparent here, since, by definition, crimes are examples of **normative** deviance and criminology is the study of crime and the social and legal responses to crimes and criminals.

- When sociologists study juvenile delinquency, they are also conducting deviance-related work.

Other deviance-related studies:
- Suicide is also a type of deviance sociology, because it entails the examination of a behavior that is, by definition, both normatively and concretely deviant in our culture.
- Researchers studying the social aspects of sexual behavior, particularly homosexuality and bisexuality, are researching in the area of deviance sociology.
  1. Anytime people talk about or investigate taboo subjects—like sexuality—they are crossing the boundaries governing the **normal** from the **abnormal**.
  2. Thus, when sexuality is studied, and particularly when this sexuality is anything other than heterosexuality, it is related to the sociology of deviance.
- Similarly, much of the sociological research in the field of AIDS also qualifies as a type of deviance sociology. This subject area is very relevant to the sociology of deviance, because people with AIDS are both
  1. **rare** from a statistical standpoint (hence, constituting concrete deviance), and
  2. **stigmatized** or **unaccepted** because of public attitudes toward their health status (hence, constituting normative deviance).
- Sociologists studying **inequality** and the effects of inequality in society are also doing work that is relevant to the sociology of deviance. These studies might include such varied topics as
  1. **racism**, **sexism**, **ageism**, and **heterosexism**, and
  2. perhaps such things as **racial** inequality and **gender** inequality.

Key 86 Functionalist explanation of deviance

OVERVIEW *A functionalist explanation of deviance contends that anytime, an act of deviance or a deviant is seen in society, that deviance or deviant exists because society needs it, him, or her to exist.*

Basic premises of functionalism: (1) Everything that **exists** in society exists because society needs it to exist. (2) Everything we **see** in society contributes in some fundamental way to the overall health and stability of the society-at-large.
- Were this not the case, functionalists argue, then these things would
  1. not have existed in the first place, or
  2. cease to exist because they will have outlasted their utility.

KEY EXAMPLE

A functionalist explanation of criminality might argue that the existence of criminals keeps many other people in society employed (police officers, probation officers, judges, defense attorneys, corrections workers).

- One reason our society may not do more to eliminate criminality is that unemployment rates would rise if crime were eradicated, and the people whose jobs would be threatened would oppose the complete elimination of criminality in society.
- A functionalist approach to crime might also contend that criminals inadvertently enable the rest of the people in society to understand more clearly where society's boundaries lie regarding appropriate and inappropriate behaviors.
- By having certain individuals who break the law, society's conformists are reminded of where our culture draws the line and what types of punishment may follow transgressions.
- The result is that some people who might consider breaking the law elect not to do so because they fear the negative consequences that they might face.

- In a roundabout way, then, the existence of deviance could help society to be more conformist overall, in spite of the deviants and their actions.

Fulfillment of cultural needs: Functionalism assumes that deviants are retained by society for a variety of reasons, all of which in one way or another relate to stability and fulfillment of cultural needs.
- Many behaviors and social phenomena that we would logically think of as being destructive to society—things like rape, prostitution, juvenile delinquency, homelessness, poverty, truancy, illicit drug use, among others—are considered **functional** under this type of theoretical paradigm.
- The goal of the functionalists is to try to explain what positive needs and functions these seemingly negative phenomena and behaviors serve in society.

Key 87   Differential association theory's explanation of deviance

OVERVIEW   *One of the most influential of the twentieth century theories of deviance has been Edwin Sutherland's and Donald Cressey's **differential association** theory. Originally, this theory was developed to explain crime and how people who once abided by the law became career criminals. In the decades since this theory was first postulated, though, it has been extrapolated to apply to other specific forms of deviance and to the broader phenomenon of deviance itself. Unlike the broad, social structural focus of the functionalist approach to explaining deviance, differential association theory takes a decidedly more **individualistic** and **subcultural** approach to explaining deviance.*

Description of differential association theory: Sutherland and Cressey phrased differential association theory in the form of **nine postulates** which, when taken together, comprise the theory's approach to understanding deviance.
- **First**, differential association theory argues that deviant behavior is **learned:** nobody is born a deviant and deviance is not an inherited trait.
- **Second**, deviance is learned in **interaction** with other persons in the process of communication.
   1. People learn how to become a deviant only when they have some sort of contact with other people who are deviant.
   2. They may watch these deviants engage in deviance or they may talk with them about deviance, or both, and thus come to understand more completely what deviance entails.
- **Third**, differential association theory states that the principal part of the learning of deviance occurs within **intimate personal groups**.   .
   1. A conformist is most likely to become deviant when interacting with deviants who are particularly well known personally,

especially if the individual feels comfortable interacting with these people.

2. In addition, deviance is most likely to occur in those individuals who develop **patterns of interaction**, as opposed to those who have only sporadic or one-time-only contact with deviants.

- **Fourth**, differential association theory states that when deviant behavior is learned, the learning includes:
  1. the **techniques** of engaging in the deviance, i.e., nondeviants must be shown specifically how to engage in deviance, because this is not always self-evident.
  2. the specific direction of **motives**, **drives**, **rationalizations**, and **attitudes**. People must be instructed about the reasons why they should deviate.
- **Fifth**, the specific direction of motives and drives is learned from definitions of the normative codes as **favorable** or **unfavorable**.
  1. People will only engage in deviance if they feel that the norms and laws governing the behaviors from which they are contemplating deviating are silly, outdated, unnecessary, or undesirable.
  2. The assumption here is that people will conform to norms and abide by laws that make sense to them.
- **Sixth**, a person becomes deviant because of an **excess of definitions** favorable to the violation of norms or laws over definitions unfavorable to the violation of these norms or laws.
  1. This, Sutherland and Cressey point out, is the principle of differential association.
  2. The assumption is that people weigh in their minds the advantages and disadvantages of abiding by norms and laws, and then engage in whichever type of behavior—**conformist** or **deviant**—they perceive outweighs the other.
- **Seventh**, differential associations may vary in **frequency**, **duration**, **priority**, and **intensity**.
  1. In this context, **frequency** refers to how often individuals find themselves deeming it more desirable to violate the laws or norms than to conform to them.
  2. **Duration** refers to the length of the time period over which individuals find themselves deeming it more or less desirable to violate or conform to certain laws or norms.
  3. **Priority** refers to the importance that the individual attaches to violating or conforming to norms and laws.
  4. **Intensity** refers to how strongly the person feels about the decision to conform or to deviate.

- **Eighth**, the **learning process** for deviant behavior involves all of the same mechanisms involved in any other type of learning.
  1. All behaviors are learned, and all are learned in essentially similar manners.
  2. Because there are certain **value judgments** at work when deviance is concerned does not mean that deviance is learned differently from any other type of behavior.
  3. *Differential association theory thus implies that people not only learn how to deviate, but also learn how to conform.*
- **Ninth**, differential association theory posits that, while deviant behavior is an **expression** of general needs and values, it is not **explained** by those needs and values, because nondeviant behavior is often an expression of the same needs and values.
  1. Needing something or not needing something is not the crucial point on which decisions to conform or to deviate hinge.
  2. Deviance and conformity involve many of the same values and needs; the decisions to deviate or to conform are often made on bases having little—if anything—to do with what people value or need.

Key 88 Labeling theory's explanation
of deviance

OVERVIEW *Unlike other deviance theories, **labeling** **theory** takes a more subjective approach to explaining deviance. Rather than believing that there is any behavior or phenomenon that is inherently deviant, labeling theory posits that there is no such thing as an **objectively** deviant person, behavior, or phenomenon. Labeling theory argues that deviance only exists when someone or some group in a position of power says that it exists. If no one labels a person, a person's actions, or a phenomenon as being deviant, then according to labeling theory, it is not deviant.*

KEY EXAMPLE

If one of your classmates came to class naked, stood atop her desk, and sang the "Star Spangled Banner" repeatedly throughout class but no one paid much attention to her or did or said anything to her about her actions (nobody **labeled** her or her actions as being unusual or inappropriate—that is, deviant), then her out-of-the-ordinary behavior could not be considered deviant according to labeling theory.

Description of labeling theory: Labeling theory utilizes a **two-by-two table**, of sorts, to determine whether someone's actions are to be considered deviant. The table's rows consist of the yes/no variable, "Did the person **engage in an act** that we would ordinarily think of as being deviant?"; the table's columns consist of the yes/no variable, "Did anyone **recognize and label** the person's actions as being deviant?" Four cells are thus formed.

- In the **first** cell, we have the **conformists**— people who did not engage in any type of behavior that might be considered deviant and whose actions were not labeled as deviant by anyone else.
- People in the **second** cell are those whom some labeling theorists have termed **secret deviants**—people who did engage in an act that would ordinarily be deemed deviant, but whose actions were

not recognized and labeled by others as deviance. In the purest labeling theory terms, this person's actions are not deviant because nobody labeled them as such.

- In the **third** cell, we have the **falsely accused**—people who did not do anything that ought to be considered deviant, but who are labeled by others around them as having done something deviant. Even though, objectively, these people have not engaged in a deviant act, under labeling theory they are considered deviants because someone in a position of power **labeled** them as such.

- The **true deviants** are in the **fourth** cell. These are people whose actions were of the sort that would typically be termed deviant, and whose actions were recognized and labeled as being deviant.

The relevance of power: Labeling theory assumes that deviance can only be created when someone or some group who has power over another person or group, wields that power and **labels** that person or group as deviant. In the **absence** of power and/or authority to apply a label of deviant successfully, deviance cannot be said to exist, according to labeling theory.

- Thus, if I as an **individual**, speaking for myself alone, say that Satanists are bizarre (deviant), that is not enough to make deviants out of Satanists because I probably do not have the power to affix such a label to an entire group of people.

- If, on the other hand, I was not alone in my quest to label Satanists as bizarre and I was able to mobilize support from other people who collectively acted to ensure that the public knew that Satanists were doing something deviant, then **together** we might be able to make Satanists deviant in the labeling theory sense.

- Power is required to create deviance; ordinarily, power is greatest when several people band together in a collective action.

Key 89 Deviance and the theory of anomie

OVERVIEW *There are two different meanings of the word **anomie**: 1) normlessness, or 2) a situation in which the existing norms are ineffective in regulating certain behaviors. Accordingly, the theory of anomie explains deviance as relating to a state of normlessness, or a social context in which the existing norms are not working well enough to regulate people's actions in that context.*

Normlessness: To say that deviance is the result of normlessness is to say that deviance occurs because there are no norms in operation in a particular situation—or alternatively, that people are completely unaware of the norms that ought to be controlling their actions in a specific context.

Example of normlessness: Imagine that someone blindfolded you, put you in a plane, flew for 16 hours without telling you where you were going, put a parachute on your back, told you how to use it, opened the plane door, and pushed you out.

- Assuming that you land safely, you find yourself in an area completely unfamiliar to you, where the local residents do not speak a language that you recognize, and where the local residents' customs are totally different from anything that you have ever seen before.
- You are essentially confronted by normlessness, because you are totally unaware of the behavioral expectations held by people in this part of the world and you are incapable of verbally communicating with the inhabitants to ask them what you should or should not do.
- Chances are great that you will do something that these people consider wrong or inappropriate—that is, **deviant.** Your deviant actions would be the result of **anomie.**

Situations in which norms are ineffective: The other meaning of anomie involves situations in which norms are present, but in which these norms are **not powerful enough** to keep people's behaviors in line with societal expectations.

Example: Drinking among college students.

- Throughout the United States, it is illegal to drink alcoholic beverages prior to the age of 21.
- Research shows that the vast majority of college students—including those aged 20 and under—drink alcohol.
- Even underage college students tend to drink on a regular basis, and often quite heavily at that.
- From a strictly legal standpoint, these people's behaviors are deviant, because they are in violation of the law, which is incapable of keeping these individuals' behaviors in check.

Conditions of anomie-related deviance: Ordinarily, when anomie-related deviance occurs, it is the result of one of two things: 1) **confusion** about what is acceptable and what is unacceptable in a particular situation, and/or 2) **lack of consensus** among societal members regarding the norms.

- Regarding confusion, if people are unclear about what they should or should not do, it will be difficult for them to conform to societal expectations at all times. In such a situation, they are likely to break norms (deviate) inadvertently at least occasionally.
- Regarding lack of consensus, if there is fairly widespread disagreement over certain norms, then people will always be deviating from somebody's expectations for their behavior; if one set of people is pleased by one's actions, then the other set of people will be displeased, and vice versa. If lack of normative consensus exists, deviance must, by definition, occur often.

GLOSSARY

acculturation The process by which people who desire to achieve cultural integration give up their "old ways" and adopt the language, customs, norms, and values of the culture of which they are trying to become a part.

achieved status Position in the social hierarchy as a result of characteristics over which the individual has some measure of personal control, such as educational attainment, criminal record, and marital status.

agents of socialization Any person or institution that teaches people about beliefs, attitudes, values, norms, or behaviors. Usually reserved for people or institutions who provide such learning frequently, for large numbers of people, on an ongoing basis.

amalgamation The process by which several groups who are simultaneously trying to gain greater acceptance in a particular culture, join forces to make their cultural assimilation process easier.

Anglo-conformity approach A philosophy under which ethnic groups in the United States are expected to abandon most of their Old World institutions, customs, and traditions in favor of those that are more obviously American.

anomie A situation in which the existing norms are ineffective in regulating certain behaviors; a state of normlessness. As a theory, explains deviance as a social context in which the existing norms do not work well enough to regulate people's actions.

anticipatory socialization Preparation for future roles using various types of role playing, whereby young people learn how they are expected to behave.

ascribed status Position in the social hierarchy that exists due to characteristics over which the individual has no control, such as sex, race, or age.

attitudes Personal evaluations or assessments, based on beliefs, about a particular person or object; how an individual feels about someone or something.

baby boom generation People who were born during the years following World War II (1945–1962); the largest birth cohort in U.S. history.

baby bust generation People born during the years after the Baby Boom (approximately mid-1960s to mid 1970s) during which there was a sharp reduction in U.S. birth rates.

baby echo generation The offspring of Baby Boomers as they begin their families, resulting in a modest increase in the birth rate in the United States.

beliefs Personal judgments about the characteristics of a particular person or object; may or may not be supported by evidence; what an individual thinks about someone or something.

closed social system A society in which class differentiations are easily identified and the lines between classes are sharply drawn. Little or no movement from one social class to another is permitted. Also known as a caste system.

concrete deviance Any characteristic, behavior, or social phenomenon that occurs so rarely that, when it does occur, it can be considered unusual. Also known as statistical deviance.

conflict theory A sociological perspective that examines systematic patterns of benefits and deprivations, patterned social struggles, and patterned competition within society to determine who systematically suffers and who systematically benefits from social inequalities.

construct A specific way to measure a given concept.

content research Investigates a tangible part of the human culture as opposed to the actual members of the culture. Usually involves some form of mass media.

convenience sampling Participants and/or phenomena are selected for study based on availability to the researcher.

core gender identity The permanent, lifelong definition of oneself as being male or female; usually determined by age 3 to 5 years.

counterculture A group that differs in its values, norms, and belief systems from, and is incompatible with the larger, dominant culture. A counterculture will attempt to change the features of the dominant culture.

cross sectional research design A study in which a group of subjects is examined once, at one point in time. Best suited to investigate relationships that are not thought to change over time or to vary as a function of age.

cultural relativism Sociological perspective that recognizes other cultures and their right to exist and have their own characteristics, values, norms, and belief systems, even if dramatically different from one's own.

cultural pluralism A cultural approach to dealing with ethnic group diversity, in which people of different ethnicities are allowed to retain their ethnic heritages and the beliefs, attitudes, values, and behaviors that come to them from their ethnic background.

cultural assimilation The process by which a particular group or subculture becomes part of or achieves acceptance by the dominant culture or society at large.

cultural integration The extent to which a particular group or subculture has become part of or achieved acceptance by the dominant culture or society at large.

culture The total way of life of a people. Includes beliefs, attitudes, values, folkways, norms, mores, laws, groups, and institutions shared by a particular society's members.

developmental socialization Process by which people apply the skills, norms, behaviors, and values that they have already learned to new situations that require adjustments to their existing ways of thinking or behaving.

differential association theory A series of nine postulates, developed to explain crime, career criminals, and deviance; states that deviant behavior and its techniques are learned through interaction in intimate personal groups. An unfavorable disposition toward norms and a favorable disposition toward the violation of norms is also learned.

ethnicity Involves a sharing of culture, cultural traits, and heritage; compare/contrast with race.

ethnocentrism The assumption that one's own way of life is the only correct way, thereby negatively judging others' ways of life.

experimental research A study design in which participants are divided into two groups, treatment or experimental and control. The treatment group is exposed to a particular situation being evaluated, the control group is not. The study compares the two groups after exposure to the given situation (treatment).

folkways Ordinary conventions or habits of everyday life. They reflect minor, generally unimportant, expected behaviors.

functionalism A theoretical paradigm to studying society examining how each part of society contributes to the overall workings of the society. Assumes that every component of society fulfills a basic need, serves a purpose, and/or contributes to the stability of the society.

gender identity formation The process by which we develop our sense of self as masculine or feminine, along with ideas about appropriate behavior, based on our maleness or femaleness.

gender inequality The systematic difference between the life experiences, social expectations, and opportunities that are available in life specifically because an individual is male or female.

gender role identity A personal belief that one should or should not act in a certain manner, based simply on whether one is a male or female.

gender The personal, social, or cultural assignment of being male or female based on labels that people apply to themselves and that most others place on them.

generalizability The extent to which a study's findings can be said to reflect the greater society or some other large social group or entity.

gerontology The scientific, holistic study of aging and the elderly.

groups A combination of people who have come together for a unified purpose or to achieve a goal, and who interact in an orderly manner.

institutional racism The systematic denial of opportunities and rewards, because of an individual's racial classification, by others in positions of power and authority.

institution A stable and widely accepted cluster of values, norms, statuses, roles, and groups that develops around some basic needs in society.

labeling theory A subjective approach to explaining deviance that states that to be deviant, a particular person, phenomenon, or behavior must be identified as such by someone or some group in power.

latent functions A term from functionalism that describes the less obvious, implicit reasons for the existence of a specific phenomenon in society.

laws Primary mechanisms of social control. Specific rules of behavior that have been formally enacted and are enforced by political authority.

longitudinal research design A group of people is examined over an extended period of time, often many years. Though costly, this method is well suited to studying how behaviors, attitudes, or phenomena change with age or over time.

manifest functions A term from functionalism that describes the explicit, outward, or obvious reasons for the existence of a specific phenomenon in society.

melting pot A cultural approach to dealing with ethnic group diversity; it assumes that much of a given individual's ethnic heritage will be lost in the assimilation and acculturation processes. The ideal person is one who is an amalgamation of many different ethnicities.

mores Social norms reflecting society's most important, cherished values. Violation of a more may be considered immoral or may entail breaking the law.

normative deviance Any behavior that runs counter to the societal expectations governing a particular social context; may involve a serious infraction violating laws or mores, or a more minor violation of a folkway or a norm.

norms Shared standards of expected behavior; similar to but with more significance than a folkway.

open social systems A society in which class differences are easily identified but lines dividing the classes are not clearly drawn. Movement from one class to another, though likely to be difficult, is possible.

operationalization The specific definition that is given for a term or the specific manner in which a concept is to be measured in a particular research study.

primary socialization Occurs early in life; the process by which basic social skills, including language and basic cultural norms, are acquired, mastered, and internalized.

qualitative research Designed to develop an overall feeling and a totalistic understanding of the phenomena at hand; rarely involves numbers; involves close hands-on or first-hand examination of given phenomena.

quantitative research Research that is numbers oriented, involving the collection of large amounts of numerical data, which is interpreted via statistical analysis.

race A way of identifying and classifying people based on specific physical characteristics passed down from generation to generation combined with the way people are categorized and treated by other people in their culture.

random sampling Participants are selected from a list of all potential subjects in a manner ensuring that each person has an equal chance of being asked to participate. Random sampling is a preferred methodology because study findings can be generalized to a larger group. Compare/contrast with convenience sampling.

reliability Refers to the reproducibility of a study's findings.

research bias Refers to problems with the representativeness and generalizability of the study such that whatever findings are obtained are rendered questionable because of methodological shortcomings in the study.

reverse socialization Occurs when someone younger, with less world experience, instills some skill, belief, or attitude into an older, more worldly wise individual.

roles An individual's responsibilities and expected behaviors within a given social situation or context.

sex The assignment of being male or female, based only on one's internal and external sexual organs.

social inequality The systematic experience of advantaging or disadvantaging certain people, which occurs on a wide-scale basis, with regularity, and along the lines of certain specific identifiable characteristics, such as gender, race, or sex.

social stratification Patterned social inequality; inequality occurring on a wide-scale basis, with regularity, and along lines of specific identifiable characteristics.

social stratifiers Traits that affect one's position in the social hierarchy.

socialization The process by which humans learn how to be and act human. The process by which individuals learn to act in groups, as family members, with peers, and in the work environment. The learning process for

norms, beliefs, attitudes, values, behaviors, and the like.

status The specific hierarchical position occupied by an individual within the social structure.

subculture Individuals or groups that share the dominant culture but also have some major differences from the dominant culture, and therefore band together for mutual support or interaction.

survey research A quantitative method based on asking specific questions, the honest and thorough answers that will allow for analysis of a given behavior or phenomenon.

symbolic interactionism A theoretical paradigm that aims to understand people's behaviors as the people themselves would uniquely interpret them.

symbol An object, sound, color, design, or behavior that represents something other than itself.

theory A coherent set of hypothetical, conceptual, and pragmatic principles forming the general frame of reference for a field of inquiry.

universal Any belief, value, attitude, characteristic behavior, norm, more, law, custom, tradition, group, or institution that is common to all known cultures.

validity Refers to how well the researcher is able to measure the social behavior or phenomenon being measured in the manner chosen to measure it.

values Indications of broad, vague, abstract goals that an individual or group has; reflected in traits that are considered worthy of respect.

INDEX